Rural Genius: Secrets to Long Term Marriages

Rural Genius Vol. 3

Hilda V Carpenter PhD

Rural Genius Copyright © 2015 Hilda V Carpenter PhD

All rights reserved.

ISBN-10: 1505602912
ISBN-13: 978-150562913

Front cover photo: W.W. and Maude Formwalt 50th Wedding Anniversary
Wearing their original wedding clothes
Photographer Unknown

For Steve

Hilda Carpenter

Rural Genius: Secrets to Long Term Marriages

Part I Husbands and Wives Tales

Too Many Experts

I did a search on Amazon.com for the top books on marriage. What I expected to see was an aggregated list for "marriage." Before I even got to that point, I discovered Amazon groups Marriage into categories! No doubt about it from Amazon's perspective Marriage is big business. The largest collection was "Marriage Counseling" with a whopping 202,013 entries. Now that's a bit inflated, since some of the books were repeated, but even so, that's a lot of books. So, I whittled down the search a bit more and asked just for "books" on "marriage counseling". In other words, I omitted dvd's.

I decided to then look for the book that had the most reviews: 4,502 reviews and touted as the # 1 Best Seller in Medical General Psychology!

It seems the authors like to add a number to the title, for example: 5 love; 7 principles; 10 steps to a—. Then there are titles that bias one or another of the genders, for example: His Needs; Her needs; Love She most desires; Respect he Desperately—

You get it.

The weirdest one I saw was touting how to save your marriage when the other doesn't want to. What the hell is that about?

If the statistic of 50% of marriages will fail is true, then why on earth does anyone get married in the first place?

Well, for me I got married because they asked me. Yes, it's true, this incredibly confident woman you see here didn't ever think

Rural Genius: Secrets to Long Term Marriages

she'd be lucky enough to get someone to ask her to marry her. So, when they did, I said, "yes." Thus, Ex #1 and Ex #2.

Aha, but I got smart after that. When Hubby asked me to marry him, I said "No." In no uncertain terms was I ever going to do that again. Well, I did. What can I say, he wore me down by asking me to marry him every day for a year. There's something to that philosophy (even though I didn't know it was a philosophy at the time). The books say, "play hard to get." Well, I wasn't playing hard to get at all, I was being bone-density honest. They sometimes say, "Don't tell all of the truth." Well, I'm as honest as a partner can get, if you have stinky breath, I'm not going to suck it up. I'm going to put the toothpaste on the damned toothbrush for you and stick it in your mouth.

But, by agreeing up front that you aren't being savvy, coquettish, shy, or insecure, you end up slowing down the courting process (which goes way too fast toward marriage). Mostly men have this delay built into their DNA. For example, Ex #1 really didn't want to get married. No doubt I harangued him to death. I manipulated with sex and every trick I could think of because my God, I was 19. I was sure no chance of marriage could come closer than Ex #1.

So, at 19 I married Ex #1 and turned 20 the next week (whew just made that old-lady deadline)! The marriage really started falling apart the second day. About 7 years into the failure/disaster he wanted to go get some counseling. Now marriage counseling can be a wonderful thing IF you have already gone through counseling on your own to understand yourself before you try to understand someone else's psyche. In my case, I was pretty much one foot out the door when we went to our local minister for help.

Hilda Carpenter

During this marvelous session with the man of the cloth (btw, the clergy are terrible marriage counselors, imho). Ex #1 talked about how awful I was while I sat there and took it. (Of course I was royally pissed, but being a woman of the South, I know how to hide my venom.) Then the clergy said, "So, Hilda, what seems to be the matter with you?"

Maybe it was a case of wording inflection, or poor grammar. He might have been intending to say, "So, Hilda, tell me your side of the story." But what I heard was: "Ex#1 seems like the perfect guy, wtf up with you, girl?"

I stared at him then Ex#1, smiled sweetly and I said, "Absolutely nothing is wrong with me." I think that was the first time that I had any clue that I could disagree with two people who were staring at me. My mother always said that I could argue with a sign post. However, I could only argue about topics, not emotions. Emotions were not allowed with my Mom, you see.

Ex #2 happened after I kicked out a "boy toy." Oh my, I didn't even have someone else lined up to take his place. I felt strangely odd — Not that I had a clue about my own psyche at this time, I just felt time-warped out of reality. I didn't know any, count 'em, any single, divorced women.

Not only did I feel divorce tainted me as a scarlet woman, but I had a little boy. I was scared. I even called my Dad and asked him what I should do. He gave me the best advice I could have ever received: "Come down here, we'll find you a place to live, job and I can help take care of the boy."

Good grief, who's going to trust that? But it was a glimmer into sanity.

I was prime for Ex #2 to sweep in and save the day. Unfortunately, I met Ex #2 within a day or two of my conversation with Daddy. I married ex #2 fast—3 weeks later. Why? Because he asked, silly! Plus, I didn't have to think, he did the thinking for me.

Stayed married to Ex #2 through another baby and the failure of his business. Oh, then about 3 months later, he left me (of course).

I had a little more resolve this time to stay single and about that time Hubby (who was a friend at the time) started sniffing around—But no WAY was I going to give in. Have sex with him? Of course, but never, never get married. It helped that the sex was off the chart good—best I had ever had. I actually didn't have to fake an orgasm. Now THIS was new! And great because I could have sex and not get married . . . THANK GOD I had some divorced friends by this time. I no longer felt like I had a misshapen nose with huge witch-warts on it. I was my own woman. Whee!!

So, what do all these experts have to say in their books? A bunch of well, bullshit. You cannot save a relationship by reading a book. Oh you can definitely get ideas about how to improve your sex life, determine if the spouse is having an affair, learn how to manipulate —But save a relationship, nah. I just don't buy it.

I think the counseling needs to be done YEARS in advance. Not into making a relationship better with someone else. Counseling needs to be about how to make your relationship with YOU better. THEN, you can most likely figure out if you want to marry, and to whom.

Regardless, and I say this particularly to women, but not exclusively so: Take Your Time. Men or women are like busses, another one will be driving by after a short wait.

Who knows, maybe that bus has a better route. And unless you have a travel guide (synonym for counselor), no one, absolutely no one can tell you the best route for you to take.

Rural Genius: Secrets to Long Term Marriages

Meet the Ex's

Over the past 44 years, I've been married three times to very different people. I reflect on this and I believe they were so different because I was at different levels of self-knowledge and immaturity. In other words, I don't blame Ex #1 and Ex #2 for the fact that it didn't work out. I just don't think I knew how to love myself. Heck, I had alcoholic parents and a highly competitive mother, it's no wonder I had skewed expectations for how a relationship was supposed to work. Probably if I had known then what I know now, I most likely would have slapped myself upside the head and waited until I was in my 30's or 40's to marry! I don't blame my parents, they did the best they could with who they were and what they had. Thankfully, during my third marriage to Hubby, I learned how to love myself—not look for someone else to make everything OK for me. Thus, our marriage has lasted a long time.

Ex #1

After my first year of college I split with the high school boyfriend who was serious, smart and had a wonderful family. I decided I needed to find the biggest party-heartier man I could find. I found him living right next door to my apartment. He was shorter than my previous boyfriends, he had brown eyes instead of blue, and he was working for Ma Bell to help his mom pay for his college, and to avoid the draft. He was a computer operator, which in those days meant he took 2 foot disks that held one megabite of people's telephone bills, manage the printers that put out the bills. All in all, in the early 1970's, it was pretty impressive. He had sandy-brown hair that always got a little greasy by day's end before his shower. And boy, he had a killer smile that was typically wrapped around a Marlboro cigarette.

Ex #1 loved to dance, I think that was the one thing that captured my heart. I'm not talking about the bodily gyrations of dancing apart, he could two-step and Western Swing better than anyone I'd ever known. In South Texas, the guys would put their arm behind the woman's neck instead of around her waist. This took a bit for me to get used to, but once I gave up the concept of ballroom dancing, I was just fine with it.

He had olive skin and sandy brown hair. I once saw a high school senior picture of him at the end of Summer and his hair was white from the sun bleaching. He skin would turn brown as mine sunburned after 5 minutes in the sun. His mom was German, I mean 1st generation, his dad was also German, but he died when Ex #1 was very young. His mom had remarried several times, so he came into our marriage with his own family baggage. Although I didn't know it was baggage at the time. I wanted to love him enough to take away his painful past (btw you cannot fix someone's past I found out later).

I'd never dated a quarterback, the quest of many young girls. While he didn't play college football, because he was short, evidently he was quite the scrambler in High School. His fans called him "worm" because he could wriggle out of any tackle. I liked that he was athletic.

Our marriage lasted 6 years resulting in our beautiful, successful son. To his credit we are still friends.

Ex #2

Ex #2 was very different than Ex #1. He wasn't athletic, he was tall, blue-eyed, and missing some teeth. He smoked Winston's—it smelled the same as Marlboro's. He was born and raised in Lubbock, Texas. He didn't dance, he smoked pot, loved going to the Gulf Coast to fish, let's see, what else, oh yeah, he owned his own business. That impressed the heck out of me! He'd been married twice before, but I never knew them or his family before our whirlwind courtship ended when we eloped 3 weeks later. That's right 3 weeks. I found out later that his second marriage was annulled, it was years later that I discovered to have a marriage annulled by a court, something pretty darn serious had happened. The records were sealed, so I never knew what happened to his second wife or their marriage.

He had a funny way of walking. My best friend said he looked like Craig Morton (Dallas Cowboy quarterback in the 1970's) when Tom Landry (Dallas' coach) would put Roger Staubach back on the field after Craig made a bad play. His shoulders were perpetually slumped forward, and tucked his chin, so he always appeared to be pouting. He had big shoulders, but they were about half the normal size because he slumped.

I left my job in a budding computer company to join him in his business. Today I still don't know why this really made his mom mad. I mean the woman did not like me at all—ever. In fact, I'm pretty sure the entire family didn't like me. They ran a 2nd hand thrift store and according to members of the family, they saw me as "uppity." Being a sharecropper farmer's daughter—I can tell you I never thought of myself as uppity. But there it was, and no matter how hard I tried to be the good in-law the dynamic never changed.

His business eventually failed and this is when I learned he was a perpetual dreamer. He thought of more get-quick-rich schemes than I ever knew existed. I went back to work in the computer industry and when he wanted to move to California, I landed a job in the Silicon Valley. He never went to work out there and was really angry with me that I made friends and loved my job. Eventually, after we had been married 5 years he had enough. He had his sister come out to help him kidnap our daughter and the three of them went back to Texas. Oh, I got my daughter back, right after he knocked me up again—this time God had pity on me and it turned out to be an ectopic pregnancy. We are still not friends, after the kind of betrayal I experienced, I learned that I didn't have to like everyone and they didn't have to like me for me to survive.

So, by the end of the two marriages, I had two kids, a great job, and friends who cared about me. As it turned out Hubby was one of those friends. I'd never been just-friends with someone before I dated him. Indeed I saw myself as a perpetual single-mother after Ex #1 and #2's adventures. That suited me fine. Now Hubby, he liked to dance, had blue eyes, a fantastic physique and was a computer genius. Oh yeah, and he wanted to marry me even though I kept saying "no." By this time, I'm 34 years old, successful in business, and making some pretty good bank.

Rural Genius: Secrets to Long Term Marriages

So, now you have the scene of a wild, first twelve years of marriage to two men. The rest I'll unfold with some really funny things that happened to me during and after all that sadness.

Long Term Marriages

In my family, people live a really long time, at least to their eighties and sometimes over 100 years old. My maternal great-grandparents, Mama and Papa, were married over 50 years. They could still wear their wedding clothes on their fiftieth anniversary. Mama had a fiery temper, and Papa was as steady as a rock. They truly loved each other, even if they didn't like each other on some days. They came from similar backgrounds and their families had similar value systems. Work hard, respect the other and know that they were together for the long haul.

Recently I've started losing my paternal aunt and uncles. It makes sense because they are in their late-eighties or early-nineties. These relatives are especially important to me because they are my Daddy's sisters and their husbands. Three of his sisters have been married to their same husband for over 40 years. I played at their houses when I was a child, and have seen them go through terribly hard times. The consistent theme is they never gave up on their marriage. I can remember my aunt saying, "Marriage is a promise. If you make a promise, then nothing will allow you to break that promise."

My father's three sisters all married his best friends. He said, "I kept losing my best friends to my silly sisters." Of course, the fact that his best friends joined his family created a loving, long-term loyalty that never ended. I think that families who grew up together and were joined by marriage had a distinct advantage. They had the chance to experience seeing and knowing each others' family values. There were really no surprises. They had

Rural Genius: Secrets to Long Term Marriages

similar tastes.

In my own experience, my first two marriages, I had never met his family before I married him. Obviously, we had different value systems that spelled doom for our relationships. In the case of hubby, I knew him for a couple of years. Thus, I met his family and spent time with them before I agreed to married him. Even though there were major differences, I could see that we had common values around money, spirituality, loyalty, kids and work ethic. These cornerstones have helped us get through some really rough times in our 30-year marriage.

At the most recent funeral of my Daddy's brother-in-law, my aunt said about her husband, "He always thanked me and said his biggest blessing was the day I agreed to marry him."

If there is any key to my relatives long-term marriage it is to know each other's values, their families' values, and maintain a mutual respect for each other. If I give thanks for the blessing that hubby came into my life, I hope that he and I will be married for another 20 years.

Hubby and I allow the concept that we will have good years and bad years, some days we won't like each other, but we will always love each other. But, the most important aspect is that our value systems align. Certainly this is what I have learned from my great-grandparents, my grandparents and my father, aunts, and uncles.

The lust leaves, sometimes love isn't readily available, but I respect hubby. We challenge each other and always check in with each other to see if there is any wedge forming that might rip us apart later.

In other words, we work at it—and it is work.

My own parents didn't make it after 25 years. My mother's rigidity and my father's infidelity spelled ruin from the beginning of their marriage. Theoretically, their families' values were aligned, but they hadn't really known each other for very long to allow discovery of their own flaws. If they had experienced each other longer, they might have been able to reconcile whether they could overcome those flaws through experiencing each other and their families. But then again, if they had realized their incompatibility before they married, I wouldn't be here. So, I guess everything works out in the end.

If I asked or sought help for my childhood traumas growing up with incompatible parents, I probably would never have Ex #1 and Ex #2. Of course, that would mean that I would not have my beautiful son and daughter. As I got healthier, I encouraged my children to deal with the traumas of their own childhood. Only time will tell if they will be able to crawl out of their adolescent bruises and into a self-sustained, healthy ability to stay the course with another person.

The Proposal

When a man asks a woman to marry him, or vice versa I guess, it's a very private and special moment, unless you are me. My first husband (in the future known as Ex#1) I harangued to death threatening to break up unless he asked me to marry him. So, instead of asking me to marry him, we went down and picked out our rings. He held off "asking" me and hid the engagement and wedding rings in the tiny boxcar in which we lived together. In the 70's this was known as "living in sin."

One day after a particular amorous afternoon in bed, I pouted and asked him, "When are you going to ask me to marry you?"

He looked down at me with his beautiful brown eyes and said, "I'll tell you what if you can find the ring, you can have it."

I'm a really good searcher because I had to hide all kids of wondrous things from my mother. Sure enough, I started getting close, and he got really, really nervous. I squeaked in delight when I saw him sweating, knowing that I was only a couple of hiding places away. That's when he reneged on the promise of "if you can find it, you can have it." I was heartbroken. I started crying to beat all cries of all womanhood that cried tears before me.

He finally relented, and gave it to me. Through puffy eyes and snotty nose, I accepted. Not terribly romantic, but we were engaged and I could finally get my mother off my back about only dating one guy.

Hilda Carpenter

My second husband (in the future known as Ex#2) was just about as romantic. We were laying on the couch watching the Red Sox (I love the Red Sox). He was holding me and gave me a sweet kiss on the cheek. He then said, "I'm going to marry you, I don't know when or where, but I"m going to marry you." No ring this time, but then again, I was, what I saw as a "tainted divorcee". Thanks mom for all those lovely images. So 3 weeks later we eloped, no ring. Oh he did buy me one about 3 weeks after the marriage, but no diamond. I figured I got what I deserved—being a divorced, tainted woman and all.

Husband #3 (in the future known as Hubby because we are still married some 30 years later) also wanted to marry me. He wanted to marry me so much that he asked me every day for a YEAR to marry him. I kept saying no, until I couldn't think of 3 reasons not to marry him. Then we drove to LA to tell his family. We stopped by the diamond district and I bought my ring—with a diamond that was dang near a carat! Wohoo! By this time, I didn't see myself as a "tainted woman" I saw myself as a liberated woman.

In case a gentleman is reading this, let me tell you, buy the ring or you will pay bloody hell for it. If she doesn't like it you can always trade it in (be sure to give her that option). Pay attention to the rings she says she likes. Oh, and if she says, "I don't really need a big diamond." Beware—she lies. All women, and I do mean all women want a big f#ing diamond.

As an example, my brother married my sister-in-law and bought her a ring with a lovely semi-precious stone in it. Want to know what she got as soon as they were married 25 years—yep, a big honking' diamond ring! Hoo-yah.

So, go in debt, take the plunge and for goodness sake get on one knee. None of mine did that knee thing. Oh well—who needs a knee when he asks everyday for a year? Not me.

Hilda Carpenter

Christmas in March

In 1984 Ex #2 and I moved to California with my two kids. Why would we leave Lubbock, TX? Well the answer isn't what you might think. He wanted to get away from all the people he owed money from the failed business. I remember him saying, "California Land of Opportunity." The problem was I was the only one earning money in my reinstated job with the computer company. I told him I could not just pull up roots and move across country without a job. With my boss' approval, I put feelers out with some of my customers to see if they might want to hire me. Sure enough, a small software company located in Cupertino, CA made an offer.

Westward ho!

As I mentioned, he was never hired by any company. He didn't want to be the stay-at-home Dad, so I paid for child care. I admit I became very surly and would arrive home from work, after picking up the kids, start dinner and he would arise from the dope-cloud to join us. I can remember caustically saying, "I saw a sign that McDonalds was hiring. Maybe you should go apply tomorrow." Yeah, I was a total bitch.

Then one day, he called me to say that he had an interview that afternoon. He said, "I might be a little late for dinner."

I gushed my excitement by saying, "No problem, I'll fix something nice for you. It'll be ready when you arrive home—whenever that is."

Rural Genius: Secrets to Long Term Marriages

So, I left work and dropped by to pick up my two kids. The day care had two separate buildings and I typically would let my son play a little longer while I gathered up my daughter. As I looked around the room for her, the care provider said, "Oh, your husband already picked her up."

My heart fell, thinking that he had either not gone on the interview, or it had gone badly. Either way, it was sure to be a dark night in our household oozing with his depression. But I kept a clear face and said, "Oh, OK, that's great. I'll see you tomorrow."

I started out to my car when the provider came out and said, "He didn't pick up your son."

…

I think I stopped breathing. I put a smile on my face and said, "Oh, OK, I'll go get him now."

I sucked up my nerves and my son and I sang and laughed all the way home. He was curious why his sister wasn't with us. I lied and said, "Oh she had a doctor appointment and will be home soon."

I opened the big door into the house and the silence hurt my ears.

I bustled my son over to the dining table and started fixing him dinner as he colored. Once he was engrossed in making me a super hero picture, I eased toward the back of the house toward my daughter's room. I winced at the creek as I opened her door.

I didn't breathe for about 2 minutes. My mouth fell as I surveyed the empty room. Her bed was gone and all the toys. Only a few little unmatched socks littered the floor. No tears, no feeling, just "snap" and I was in a mode of protecting my son.

I returned to the kitchen and continued preparing our dinner. I noticed there were two envelopes on the counter with Ex #2's script. One had my name, the other my son's. I opened the letter addressed to me. A $250 check floated onto the counter. No note. I slashed open my son's and read words that explained why he couldn't take him with them. Legally he was not his son, he could only take his sister.

I turned and finished cooking the meal, rote movements drove me through the process. Then suddenly my son looks up and he said, "He took her didn't he?"

I decided even though he was much too young to face such trauma, there was no way I could lie to him. "Yes, honey, he did."

On my last day on earth I will remember those little shoulders dropping and his chest holding his chin. I ran over to him and we both cried. I said, "I will get her back. I promise."

For 4 days I had no idea where they were. I kept calling his mother asking if she had heard from him. "No, we don't know anything."

I confided my horror story to my friend. She had been married to a lawyer, so she called him for advice. Her ex husband said that I must file for divorce immediately.

"Why?"

"Because you could lose your daughter if you do not take action. The courts will see it as you didn't care enough to go after her."

He connected me to a lawyer in Texas, who said the same thing. He also told me his retainer fee was $2,500. I know I paled because my friend was afraid I was going to faint. After I hung up the phone, telling him I would get the money somehow, I asked her what could I do? I had $37.23 in my bank account. The $250 check Ex #2 left would not come close to covering his $657 phone bill. Evidently he'd been calling home, a lot.

I called my Mom to ask for a loan of the $2,500. She said, "No."

"Do you realize I could lose custody of my daughter, YOUR granddaughter?"

"You need to come home and take care of this."

"I will, but I have to take some steps, two lawyers said if I don't file that I will lose her."

"No, I won't help you."

So much for motherly love.

One friend said she could loan me $500. My boss, to whom I'd also confided, said he would loan me $1,000. Son had a savings account that had $1,000. I had the money. I told Son, my Boss, and my friend that I would pay them all back on a monthly basis.

I sent the check to the lawyer on Thursday, two days after they had disappeared. On Friday, I called his parents again.

He answered.

It was then that I got mad, I mean like seeing red mad. "How dare you not call me to say she was alright, or where you were. I had no idea where you were for 4 Fricking days! I am a wreck. Why did your parents not call me to say you were OK?"

"She's just fine. I don't know why they didn't call."

All I could do was swallow. Then, "I want to speak with her. NOW."

"She's asleep. It's 2 hours later here, remember?"

"Tell her Mommy called."

Two weeks later was Christmas. I boarded the flight with my son, it was his turn to go spend Christmas with his Dad. As soon as I had him safely with Ex #1, I called Ex #2.

Rural Genius: Secrets to Long Term Marriages

"I'm coming over and I expect Daughter to be there."

I was staying with my mom and step-dad, yes the same ones who would not loan me the money. But what was I to do? I certainly wasn't going to stay with his parents—his mother hated me. I asked to borrow their car, and they blessedly said, "Yes."

My daughter had not seen me for 2 weeks. In childhood development terms when a 2 year old is separated from her mother for 2 weeks, it spells a disastrous emotional setback. Sure enough, she was so shy, she acted like she didn't quite know who I was. I tried to hold back my tears, but they were leaking. Ex #2 must have taken pity on me because he picked her up and brought her to me. When she fell into my arms, I smelled her hair, her face, I kissed her eyes, cheeks, chin and forehead. "My baby." was all I could utter.

I put her to bed, then joined Ex #2 in the kitchen. We drank tea and talked. Eventually, all the emotional stress culminated in his bed. I called my parents to tell them I was staying over at his house.

The next morning after another lovemaking, I asked him, "I have been wondering something. How on earth did you drive across the country by yourself with a 2 year old? I mean, we had trouble getting from Texas to California with both of us wrestling her."

"I wasn't alone."

SNNNNAAAAAAPPPPP

Hilda Carpenter

"What do you mean you were not alone. Who was with you?"

"My elder sister."

SSNNNNNNNNAAAAAAPPPPP

"You mean the entire time I was calling all your family, hysterical with fear, they all knew?"

"Of course."

I calmly arose from his bed, turned my naked body toward him and said, "I will be going back to California and I am taking her with me."

"Don't you want to go with us over to my folks home for Christmas."

"No, I don't think I'd feel comfortable with that at all. I expect you to bring her and all her things over to Mom's this afternoon. We have a flight out tomorrow. If you want to come back to California, get a job and try to make this work, then OK. Otherwise, I'm filing for divorce and I will keep my children with me."

My son and daughter flew back with me. My friends were there to pick us up. A few months later I had reinstated my son's savings account, paid back my boss and my friend. Then the IRS showed up at my work. Ex #2's failed company was liable for

$3,652 and someone had to pay. Ex #2 said he wasn't going to pay for it. He said I should just ignore it.

I said, "They will garnish my wages, won't you help pay for it?" He didn't, I paid it over 6 months.

The following month after the IRS visit, during a business lunch with my friends, I said, "I hate Christmas."

They all loved the holiday and asked me why I was so Scrooged about Christmas.

"Well, let's see, I didn't get one present last year. Oh wait, that's not right, I won back my daughter."

"What did your parents get you?"

"Nothing."

"Your kids?"

"They are 7 and 2, are you kidding?"

The business lunch went on and I dropped the subject. I mean I didn't want to be the pitiful person. I had my family back, who needed wrapped presents.

A few weeks later, Hubby (then just my friend) came by the house with his kids to play with mine. He said, "I have something for you."

Hilda Carpenter

"What's that?"

"A Christmas present. But it's really hard to find Christmas wrapping in March."

He handed over a box with Easter wrapping. "For you. Because no one should *not* get a Christmas present."

I started laughing, tears pouring over my eyes. I had no idea someone could be this nice.

"Yeah, that's me, that nice guy." He smirked.

I tore through the wrapping to discover a beautiful Waterford bud vase. Then he pulled a yellow rose from behind him. "For the Yellow Rose of Texas."

"Yellow roses mean friendship, you know." I laughed.

"I'll always be your friend." His blue eyes sparkled.

Rural Genius: Secrets to Long Term Marriages

Winning the Divorce Story

Right after I moved to California, Ex #2 left to return to Texas. It was his idea to move to California after bankrupting his business along with all my savings, but I guess he decided the Golden State wasn't right for him. The only problem was he stole our daughter right out from under my nose.

To say the least we didn't stay together after that fiasco. I did get my daughter back a few weeks later, thank God.

Well, I made friends with several people at the company that hired me. We would all go out, with kids, and have lots of adventures. There was one friend that we all called the "hunk" because he was absolutely beautiful, but he was surly and a real jerk.

I couldn't see what all my friends liked about him, but we all palled around together, so I tagged along even when the hunk was there. I did like his kids, though.

Oftentimes we would all go out to lunch together. This was tons of fun because we would usually order a bottle of wine to go with our meals.

One time on such an occasion, for whatever reason, we all started talking about how awful our divorces were. All my pals were divorced, including the hunk. Well, one by one we decided we needed to judge who had the worst divorce story.

When it came my turn I related the disaster of Ex #2 stealing my daughter and the effort to get her back. I was top of the hill as all my friends said, "Yeah, you got me beat." We took another swallow of wine and toasted.

Then the "hunk" said, "Nah, yours is nothing compared to mine."

Well, the ohs and ahhs came out at that point. But he wouldn't relate the story. After we all chided him for being chicken, he at last agreed to tell what had happened. Now my friends had known the hunk for a lot longer than I had, but I was surprised that he hadn't confided his story to them before now.

We all listened as he started the saga.

"My wife was cheating with an architect."

"Oooo."

"No," he responded, "that's not it. She later moved down in her selection to have an affair with a hot-dog roller at the local mall."

"Uuuhhhgggg." we all cooed at his tale.

"No," he baited us, "that's not it. One day, after we had separated, she asked me if I could pick up some prescriptions for the kids on my way home from work. As I picked up the prescriptions the pharmacist said 'I'm sorry but birth control pills are not covered on your health insurance.' And then continued to tell me how much I owed." He stopped his tale.

Silence, we waited for the next shoe to fall. He didn't say anything.

I said, "Oh my God you had had a vasectomy."

Rural Genius: Secrets to Long Term Marriages

He pointed his index finger at me and said, "Bingo."

He won the divorce story contest hands down.

I looked at him with a new eye, one with some understanding of why he was so distrustful, so surly. He went up a gazillion percent in my book.

He truly was a hunk.

Talking about our pasts, without reserve, put both of us on a path of self-healing. The Hunk, later became Hubby, but that's a different story.

Hilda Carpenter

Honeymoons

I don't know how most honeymoons go, but I have had three, so I'll give it a go and say I know a good honeymoon from a bad honeymoon. A honeymoon is supposed to be that magical time when two newly-married people escape from all they know (people and places) to fully experience each other and set the tone for their (they are sure) long-term marriage.

So, let me tell you how not to do it. Then you can figure out how to make it successful, because honestly, I have no clue.

Honeymoon #1:

I married when I was 19. Yeah that's a real stumbling block to a good honeymoon. Why? Because I was still a kid and hadn't experienced traveling to exciting places, much less special foods.

I grew up in dusty old West Texas. We only had beef (it was good mind you), potatoes, brown iceberg lettuce, beans, cornbread, and my grandmothers' fantastic home made rolls.

I prayed that my first husband wasn't drunk when I walked down the aisle. Sobriety when making a life-commitment is celebration enough for a good honeymoon, right?

My future husband was sober, but terribly hung over. I'm quite sure the best man was still drunk. I could always tell if my husband was sober because when he was drunk he had one eye that would point to the wall, the other one tracked—slowly.

If you like alcohol and want every one to have a great time, then

Rural Genius: Secrets to Long Term Marriages

have champagne at your reception with lots of dancing.

I didn't do that. I had my reception catered by the lovely women of the First Presbyterian Church in the reception hall. The reception hall was a linoleum, white walled, room with folding chairs and long tables. Oh don't get me wrong, those ladies could cook a good cake and pour punch. That's right, we didn't have a meal.

Then we drove a gazillion miles to Carlsbad Caverns and stayed in the Holiday Inn. Oh yeah, that's a lot of fun, staring into the sun for 3 hours, then arriving at a tiny town with an old bed that smells like an old bed — yes we did have the honeymoon suite, which meant that we had a couch in addition to the bed, tables, 2 chairs. You get the picture. Oh yeah, and I don't know how it is now, but back then Carlsbad Caverns was dry—meaning they didn't sell alcohol. I have to face my wedding night with my new husband sober. That can be a real wake-up call. We always partied hard, so we had mostly been buzzed when we interacted.

Next, I went into the tiny bathroom and change out of my going-away-clothes (that's what you change into after you take off the wedding dress after the reception). I took a long bath, then rubbed lotion all over my body so he will know I put out some effort. I even shaved my legs for the second time that day. I pulled my beautiful nightgown out of my suitcase to shake the wrinkles out of it.

Then I spent the next 20 minutes flicking rice off my lotion-ey, guey body. Yes, my bridesmaids thought it would be funny to dump a box of rice in my suitcase. I didn't notice the rice before I shook the damned night gown.

Hilda Carpenter

Finally, I opened the door and was swept away by my husband into the bed. Well, after a long, hot 3 hour drive where the air conditioner sporadically worked, and I had a migraine from staring into the sun. Maybe we just did it and fell asleep.

The next day we went to see Carlsbad Caverns, only I noticed it was not the magical place it was in the 1950's, but an over-commercialized, crowded, smelly dump. The stalactites and stalagmites were still pretty impressive.

Now that I had the wedding night, main attraction over with, we drove to El Paso and stayed in another Holiday Inn. The drive wasn't so bad from Carlsbad, so I still had lots of energy (I mean after all I was only 19)! He said there was nothing to really do in El Paso. For entertainment we trekked over the boarder to Juarez. We took in strip shows and listened to some guy yell all night "Do you want to see the Tomatoes? Do you want to see the Monkey?"

Nothing like listening to your new husband whistle at the strippers on stage.

We drank a lot, no more than that. We stumbled back to our hotel. I realize that my husband is not in the mood because he's throwing up in his shoe on the floor.

Next, we drove 8 hours from El Paso to Beeville, Texas to go see his mother in her trailer house. It's my birthday, so I figure they are probably going to take me out to celebrate turning 20.

Nope. No presents, no dinner, we sat in front of the TV. To be polite, I stifled my gags from all the cigarette smoke. I really tried not to stare at her lips, 'cause she doesn't wear her teeth at night.

Rural Genius: Secrets to Long Term Marriages

I cried myself to sleep and thought, "What the Hell have I just done?" I had not really learned to cuss, so I had not learned the appropriate time to use the "Frick" word. But now was a good time to start.

Honeymoon #2:

It's been a whole 2 years since my divorce. My kid and I live in a dark, tiny apartment inconvenient to everything, but it's cheap. I fed my boy well, I ate popcorn and drank rum and coke for dinner.

Then, through my job I met the president of a company! Wow, things are looking up. He's tall (Ex #1 was not tall) Yay! But he doesn't like to dance (Ex #1 at least liked to dance).

In 3 weeks he swept me off my feet so much that I agreed to marry him that weekend. Yes, rather than running him through my family, I eloped. Then, we went to work the next day, I mean yes, work. Take kid to day care and life is normal. BUT we both agreed to get away for a week for a honeymoon.

Everything is set, the jeweler has called to say our wedding rings are ready. It's about time, I mean we've now been married 4 weeks, longer than we knew each other before I married him.

I threw a temper tantrum because he didn't want to stop to get our rings before we hit the road. Yes, we're driving 11 hours to Santa Fe.

At 4 am, I decided that I couldn't drive any longer because I am so sleepy. He's been asleep in the shotgun seat of the car for hours, but he's pretty stoned, so best not to let him drive.

We check in to a Holiday Inn in Albuquerque. We slept until the manager is pounding on our door at 3 pm the next day.

We can't stay in to enjoy each other, because we only checked into the room for 1 day and they need to clean it for the next guest. My husband is pretty surly, because he hasn't gotten stoned yet. But, I'm in love so I overlook his tiny faults.

We drive 3,000 miles up the Western Slope of the Rocky Mountains. When I take over driving from him I noticed there is strange flaking stuff at the left side of the base of the seat on the leather. I ask him what it is. He just shakes his head and shrugs his shoulders. The next time he drives I noticed him picking his nose and rubbing the residual on the side of the seat.

Gag.

I wouldn't drive anymore.

After the long round-trip journey, we returned home. Returning to my child from marriage #1 is the best part of the honeymoon.

Honeymoon #3

I'm scared shitless of getting married again. But, he has asked me every day for a year, yes every day, to marry him. He finally asks me to give him 3 reasons why I won't marry him. I look at him and say Ex #1 and Ex #2. But I can't come up with another reason, because he really is a good guy. Do I love him? What the frick do I know? Yes, by this time I learned the appropriate time to use the word "Frick."

Rural Genius: Secrets to Long Term Marriages

I laid out some expectations for the honeymoon. I didn't want to take the 4 kids that we have between us. He agreed that was fair. I wanted to go someplace I had not been before. He agreed that was more than fair. Then I give him the final test and say, "I want to go skiing." He stops for a minute and says, "I don't know how to snow ski." I smiled, knowingly mind you, and said, "I know. You can learn."

I figured I had him…nope he agreed. What…the…frick? So I'm sunk now. My final ace in the hole: "I want champagne, dinner and dancing at the reception."

He grinned broadly, blue eyes dancing and said, "Of course!"

Since it's my third time around none of my family except my 2 kids from the previous two marriages show up. My mom said, "The proof is in the pudding." And hangs up the phone. I was impressed that all of his family showed up and were really excited. His dad was even going around with the champagne bottle making sure that everyone's glass stayed full.

I threw the bouquet (I didn't have to change because by this time, I had figured out to wear the going away dress at my wedding AND reception). My friend kept my kids and we ran by the apartment we've been living in for 2 years to pick up the bags. We screwed like bunnies because we had plenty of time before the plane takes off!

Holy cow, we're going to FLY somewhere!!!??? This is good. In my mind's eye I was seeing beautiful rocky mountains and long, luxurious snow slopes to ski. A fireplace bar for apres-ski drinks. As we get to the airport I see that we are NOT getting on

American, or even Air France, we're going to board Southwest Airlines for Reno.

"WHAT—THE—FRICK???" I don't think this, I actually said it to him. I was pissed.

He holds up his arms in defense and says, "We're renting a car there and will go up to Tahoe."

I was no longer pissed.

He rented the car. Unfortunately, there have been heavy snow falls that would rival the Donner party. The Highway Patrol tells us that we need to affix chains on the tires. Or, we can pay $5 to have someone else put the chains on the tires. He had no cash.

WHAT—THE—FRICK?

I was pissed again.

Thankfully, the rental car came with chains in the trunk. I sat there waiting for him to get out and put the chains on. I mean after all, I donned my going away suit after we screwed each others brains out at the apartment. I still wore my cute little shoes (because I didn't know I was going to get snow bound).

He doesn't ski, so he doesn't know how to put the chains on.

WHAT—THE—FRICK???

I step out into the snow with my open-toed shoes to put the chains on the damned car. My little cotton coat doesn't help hold in my body heat, but I didn't get cold, because I'm so mad, my anger kept me warm.

We arrived in Tahoe around 10 pm. Starved.

He took me out to a fantastic Italian restaurant and we drank about 3 liters of wine.

That's better.

We returned to the condominium he rented for the honeymoon. Since we screwed that afternoon, we are both exhausted and fall into bed asleep.

Rather than awakening slowly and luxuriously for a day of snow play, he awakens me at 7 am.

WHAT—THE—FRICK!!??????

I told my dear husband that I have never been, will never be, and don't even want to be a morning person. He ignores me, and he's like this little puppy dog talking about ski lessons.

I figure, OK, well while he's in bunny class I'm going to ski some black diamonds and have a Hell of a time.

He says, "You aren't going to take a lesson with me?"

WHAT—THE—FRICK???? He was never this needy before. But, I wanted to get the honeymoon back on track. Smiling I purr, "Of course I'll take a lesson, but we'll probably have different classes, because I know how to ski." He couldn't argue this.

Hilda Carpenter

So, we head out, rent boots, skis, poles and oh yeah, buy an overpriced parka because my coat is from the going away suit. Damned suit. I'm going to burn it when I get back home.

Lining up for class selection, he is immediately chosen for the bunny class. I get a private lesson. Sweet.

At noon, I skied on down and started looking for him among the thousands of milling skiers.

I almost didn't recognize him because he was holding on to his skis standing at the bottom with a "I hate skiing" look on his face.

Determined to keep things light, I say, "How was your lesson?" with a cheery voice.

"I failed bunny slope." He grumbles.

Oh shit.

I tell him, "It's OK, we can sit in the bar or go play in the snow."

"No, I told you I was going to give you a ski vacation for our honeymoon. We are going to ski."

Now one of the reasons I liked him and agreed to marry him was his competitive nature. We agreed to go on the green slopes to practice his skiing.

There is a reason he failed bunny slope.

Day 2 of honeymoon: He took another lesson and improves enough to ski with me—if we take it s-l-o-w.

Rural Genius: Secrets to Long Term Marriages

Day 3 of honeymoon, he says, "We have to leave early this afternoon to catch our flight."

Flight? Day 3? WHAT—THE—FRICK!!!"""

Yes, the honeymoon lasts exactly 3 days. We arrive back into Reno to turn in the car when he realized he's left his billfold in the locker back up in Tahoe.

Yeah, honeymoons are not my forte.

Since I'll never get married again (been married to Hubby for nearly 30 years now), I can tell you what not to do on a honeymoon. But I can tell you what to look for in a husband:

He knows how to be sober.
He is socially graceful and likes to meet your friends.
He likes to dance to show you off.
You know he's not a obnoxious nose picker.
He has a good job with reliable job attendance.
He is smart.
He comes from a good family who adore you.
You've been with him in trying times and you still like him.

Because the honeymoon is just the start of the discovery process. Good luck, oh and learn how to say "Frick" at the appropriate times. It helps.

Once you have all that, the honeymoon really doesn't matter. And if things go haywire on the honeymoon like #3 did for me, it makes for great stories that you can both laugh about through the hard years.

Hilda Carpenter

Hubby and I have been married nearly 30 years. Not bad.

Rural Genius: Secrets to Long Term Marriages

"The Revolving Door is Me" Epiphany

I married very young, too young to know I was too young. Let's face it when you are young, all you want to do is be independent from the ropes that hold you back from finding your identity. For most people, they go to college, live away from Mom and Dad, then eventually graduate, get jobs, live on their own, then get married.

In the process of severing the ropes of childhood, a person conceivably grows up. "Up" being the operative word. I know some people who are in their 70's who have still not grown up. What I mean is they still act like adolescents or children. They are looking for an easy path, someone to help them—or blame.

I think it's the blaming that indicates whether you have grown "up" or not. In my case, I had a lot of people I could blame. Hell, my parents drank like fish, and I don't mean water. My mother really didn't like me the best, no it's true. She even was able to tell me that when I got into my late 50's—it was a wonderful affirmation in a very weird way.

I had Ex #1, who in my mind "stole" me from my ropes of childhood. Then I had Ex #2, who stole my daughter. Yeah, there was a lot of stealing going on in my little head. My parents stole a normal childhood.

I was just a poor little girl that everyone liked to steal from (key phrase here is "little girl").

After two failed marriages, I met Hubby. He was charming, sometimes a royal jerk, but incredibly handsome and great in bed.

Hilda Carpenter

What more was there to ask? He didn't steal anything from me. In fact, he contributed to the overall living expenses, fixed my car, did chores like laundry, bathrooms, etc. I finally found someone who didn't steal from me. I was free to grow "up."

I would often complain to Hubby about mom, Ex #1 or Ex #2. He sympathized, because his kids had been stolen from him too during a truly nasty divorce. Boo hoo. We were the victims. Hubby used to always say, "Yeah, I'm a nice guy and I finished last." I couldn't have agreed with him more, except I was the nice guy in my scenario.

One Christmas we loaded up the kids to go visit my parents (his parents had already gone to their great reward, so I didn't have to put up with the in-laws who disliked me as I'd had to with Ex #1 and Ex #2). I looked over at him as the airplane descended and said, "OK, my mom's going to comment on me in the following order before we get 15 minutes from the airport on the drive to their house. Weight, hair, job."

Hubby kind of shushed me, "She can't be that bad, she had you."

Definitely a nice guy—but he hadn't met her yet, either.

I said, "Just wait and see."

So, we pile into the car, Mom and Dad in the front, Hubby, me and my 2 kids in the back. It takes about 30 minutes to get to my folk's house. They live in Lubbock, TX. If you have ever heard the song by Mac Davis, "I thought Happiness was Lubbock, Texas in the Rearview Mirror," it couldn't be a truer story to me.

Hubby looked over after we got into the car and mouthed, 'I-T-'S

Rural Genius: Secrets to Long Term Marriages

F-L-A-T'

To which I stifled a giggle.

About that time, mom pulls down her windshield visor that has the little lighted mirror, so she could look at me. "Why Hilda, you've put on a little bit of weight, haven't you? Bless Your Heart. I'll have to be sure not to cook the candied yams! But I love what you are doing with your hair. Are you coloring it now? So, tell me are you still working all those long hours? It's so hard on the kids and Hubby, I know."

As she was talking, I held up my fingers against the back of her seat, never taking my eyes off of her while she talked. One, two, three the fingers went up. After she got done with me, she started chatting with the kids asking them about school, babysitters, etc. I glanced over at hubby and he had his mouth open looking at his watch. 9 minutes 17 seconds. A new record. Bless Her Heart.

Well, this is not really about my mother. This woman, by all standards, is a great woman, loved by all, including me. Rather it's what happened after we got to my folks big rambling ranch house.

You see when you get divorced and you have a child with your ex, it means he gets to see them on a specific periodic basis. So, Ex #1 comes along and picks up child #1. About 30 minutes later, Ex #2 comes along and picks up child #2. It was weird.

I walked into the big kitchen where Mom, Dad and Hubby were waiting. I needed a stiff drink. To this, my mother was most accommodating, Bless Her Heart.

Hilda Carpenter

I turned to Hubby … and immediately called him an old boyfriend's name.

He looked at me and said "you mean, #####?" (# = Hubby's name in case you couldn't figure that out).

I gasped. Had I really called him by the wrong name? Oh — my — God!! Turning beet red, I apologized profusely and took the double martini that Mom (god love her soul) handed me.

It was then that I had a vision—if you believe such things. I'll call it an incredible moment of clarity, an epiphany.

I realized I had all these men traipsing through my life — lots of awful stories — and the one constant through all those stories was me.

I looked at my mother no longer with blame. I smiled at Hubby realizing I had a really good man by my side.

I was the one that needed work, to patch up that revolving door and be responsible for my own happiness.

No more blame. Just me. OK, I can do this — is there a manual somewhere that tells you how?

Rural Genius: Secrets to Long Term Marriages

Tools

Now I admit, most men are the tool buyers in their family, and ours is no different. Hubby probably buys about 1/2 more tools than I do. So naturally the Home Depots and Lowes most always have men working in the aisles. Thus, continuing the stereotype.

I think if they had big-busted women in the aisles, more men would ask for help when they are looking for whatever gadget they need to purchase. In fact, I'll bet if these stores hired big-busted, blonde women, they would double their traffic into the stores—which would result, more than likely, in more sales.

Alas, I'm not the CEO of either company, so the tradition continues of hiring little old men in the aisles. I don't mind that though, I like little old men. I especially like the snarly ones.

One day, Hubby and I decided to buy a weed trimmer. This was right after we moved to the country and learned about the speed that wildfires can travel. We were advised by our neighbors that we needed to trim the field of three-foot weeds growing in our pasture. I had to agree with them, since we don't have any four-legged stock to eat the weeds/grass.

We walked into one of these big-box hardware stores and were sidetracked by all the shiny, new bar-b-que contraptions. Hmm, we needed one of them too. My husband long-ago hung up his BBQ tools when he discovered I could not beat his kitchen-cooking, but I was hell on wheels with the BBQ. So, I do all the BBQ-ing in our family.

After looking at all the features and fending off the BBQ salesman

Hilda Carpenter

(who naturally only talked to my husband), Hubby happened to mention that we were really there looking for a weed trimmer.

I was still looking at the side burners and lights, timers, oh heck you name it. I turned to speak to my husband and he was gone.

After searching through the 10,000 square feet without finding him, I asked a man to go check the mens' room for me. Nope, not there either.

Damn.

So, I decided to totally embarrass him by having him paged on the loudspeaker. The women check-out people said, "It happens all the time." Another stereotype: women losing their husbands in a hardware store.

He came up front with a spiffy weed eater and the smiling, ever-so-helpful little, old man. The old man said, "Women never like coming to these stores, you know."

I was absolutely incensed—What did he mean? I LOVE coming to these stores and protested loudly at his assumption. He just chuckled and said, "Of course you do, ma'am."

Hubby ignored my rant (he's heard it all before, numerous times) and got in line.

Then I was mad at Hubby! He didn't even show me his find, or the features of the weed eater before making his choice.

I said, "I wanted to help pick it out!"

Rural Genius: Secrets to Long Term Marriages

Acting as if he didn't know what I was talking about, he just said, "We got a good weed eater." But he didn't tell me WHY it was a good weed eater. I got madder.

"I lost you! I had to page you! In fact, you DUMPED me to go off with that other guy." My voice raised the eyebrows of several men standing in line around us. This made me even madder. I was beginning to sound like an operatic coloratura. Somehow, I couldn't help myself. The assumptions, the stereotypes plus getting dumped at the BBQ just pissed me off.

But mostly what pissed me off was the little old man's assumption that I didn't buy tools. I'll bet if a big-busted, blonde had offered to help Hubby find the weed eater, he would have at least thought twice (he's a very faithful man) before leaving me with the BBQ pit.

Hell hath no fury than a woman dumped for a little old man.

Hilda Carpenter

Lawn Mowers

Hubby and I bought some country property in Texas when we retired from our jobs in California. We built a house bigger than the one we'd raised our 4 kids in. Why? Because I wanted big rooms and plenty of rooms for the kids to come visit. Do they come? No, but that's another story.

We also have a really big space around the house that requires mowing. After asking around, we discovered that there was this specialty store that focused on yard maintenance for large lots.

Wohoo!

So, we trek into the store and start looking at mowers.

There were about 20 different types of mowers. Mowers that had gears to help the operator push or back up with one finger. Nice. There were electric, gas-powered mowers, mowers with shredders built in, so we didn't have to rake afterward. There were large ones, small ones, green, orange, red, blue. I mean there were more mowers than I had ever seen piled along the wall of this store. They even had them stacked vertically. All price tags showed prominently, if price was a consideration in the purchase.

Now, in the middle of the showroom, there were the ride-on mowers. These came in red, orange and green. They had steering wheels or sticks. You could get a cover for them if you didn't want to get sunburned while cutting the weeds. Some had a beer holder, in case you wanted to imbibe while "working". Some of the mowers could even turn in really tight circles to help you get around trees.

Rural Genius: Secrets to Long Term Marriages

I started sitting on all of the various types of mowers, I figured seat comfort had to come into play as much as beer holders and umbrellas. I mean, Hell, if you're going to sit down to mow the lawn, why would you sit on a hard seat? Then I found a mower that you could stand up to mow the lawn, but you didn't push the mower, you rode on it standing up. I just laughed at that, if you were going to mow the easy way (meaning if you weren't going to push it)—why on earth would you stand?

Then I sat on a red one that had two sticks for each of your arms. I had seen these on the side of the road where the professional cutters cut the weeds and grass alongside the public roads.

I told my husband (he was still over looking at the push mowers) that if we were going to buy a mower, we should get what the professionals use.

The salesman asked how many acres we had to mow. I said, "3". My husband said "1/2" at the same time. The salesman looked confused.

Then my husband went on to say that we had about a 1/2 acre around the house to mow. I chimed in that it also had lots of trees to get around. Plus, I noted to him that the other 2.5 acres had to be mowed too. He nodded his head comprehending my point.

"Have you ever had a ride-on mower before?"

"Nope." (At least Hubby and I gave the same answer to that one).

"Well, why don't you try it?"

Hilda Carpenter

I'm in!

So we went out back and he brought out the type of mower I'd been sitting on last, the one with the two sticks and comfortable chair.

"Who's going first?"

I said, "Well, he'll probably be the main one cutting the lawn, but I also can do it."

OK, he started explaining all the features to Hubby and I attentively watched and listened.

"This drives like a tank. What I mean is if you push both of these levers at the same time, the mower moves forward. If you pull them back at the same time, the mower moves backward. Now, if you want to turn left, you push the right one forward and pull the left one back. If you want to turn right, you push the left one forward and pull the right one backward. If you want to go in reverse, you pull both back, but if you want to turn when you are going backward, you put one lever forward or back, depending on which way you want to turn. Going backward, everything is reversed. If you want to back up to the right of center, you push the left lever forward, and vice versa for left—push the right forward."

Clear as mud.

"How do I stop?" I asked.

The salesman looked at me (I knew I had scored points when I asked such a smart question). Then he said, "Have you ever

Rural Genius: Secrets to Long Term Marriages

driven a standard shift?"

Hmmph. "Of course I have, I learned how to drive on a tractor when I was 8 years old."

He smiled. (Score more points for the little lady).

"OK, then you simply take both levers back to neutral in the middle."

Simple.

So, Hubby is sitting on the mower when he turns it on. "Oh yeah, it will also stop when you aren't sitting on the seat."

Hubby quickly swung his face toward the salesman. "Why would I not be on the seat?" I could tell he was nervous. He doesn't like to fail in front of other people. Most men don't.

"Well, if you flip the mower, it'll stop."

I started laughing.

Hubby said, "Great." In a very flat voice, I might add. He wasn't finding the answer funny at all.

It was time…

Hubby very gently pushed the levers forward and started creeping along. He followed the instructions to turn right, then left, still creeping along at 1 mph.

Salesman said, "Go ahead and go around that big berm out there.

Hilda Carpenter

Drive it out, round the berm, then head back and stop."

I was practically jumping up like a bimbo cheerleader telling him to put on the gas!

He pushed the levers oh-so-little forward and began a very creeping pace. He never did get it pushed out all the way in order to keep control of the mower. I kept yelling for him to go faster, but by this time he was about 1/4 mile away and couldn't hear me anymore. He s-l-o-w-l-y rounded the berm and made it back to the salesman and me.

"My turn!" I yipped!

Practically pushing hubby off the seat, I climbed on. The salesman started repeating all the instructions, but after 2 words, I was gone. Full out pushed those levers as far as they would go.

Man that mower can go fast!

I got to the berm and slowed enough to make the round around it. Then I pushed the levers way out again. I was going to set the track record for going around that berm, about 1/2 mile total circle start to end.

The wind was blowing my short, blond hair back, like a woman in a novel riding a fast horse. There was only one problem.

I have really, really huge boobs. No really, they are huge— gargantuan you might say. You've seen these girls jogging with their little sports bras? Well, my sports bra first of all makes me look like I've got uni-boob with a huge butt crack sticking out. Plus, my sports bra in no way keeps the boobs still like the little-

Rural Genius: Secrets to Long Term Marriages

boobed women's. I flop. So, I don't run, it's that simple.

Ok, so on the ride back I'm laughing like a hyena. Yes, it was that much fun to go fast on that mower, (and the seat was comfortable) but that wasn't why I was laughing. The field had been dug up and there were lots of pits and bumps. My boobs were flopping so high as to slap my chin. With each bump—WHAP—boob punch to the chin. I could see myself in the expressions of hubby and the salesman trying not to laugh, and looking anywhere but my boobs. That made it that much funnier. When I get tickled, I simply cannot control not laughing. The more I laughed the harder it was to slow down.

They started scrambling as I got about 10 yards from them laughing like a crazy person. I finally was able to stop snorting (yes I snort when I get really tickled) enough to take my hands off the levers. Poof, the levers automatically return to neutral (Did he say that before? I can't remember).

Tears are streaming out of my eyes. My hair is standing out in all directions—I look like I've been electrocuted.

Hubby says, with all concern, "Are you all right?"

I nearly fall off the tractor laughing at that. I know he's seen my boobs for many years, but I'm quite positive he has never before seen me boob-slap myself.

Hubby walked back into the showroom shaking his head and bought the push mower.

Hilda Carpenter

Wrong Tool for the Job

Did I tell you Hubby and I bought a push mower? Well we did. It was a big step up from the electric mower we had in California that we used to mow about 10 square yards. Hubby said after we bought the gas mower that he really needed to apologize to our son for not getting one before now. You see Hubby's dad had an electric mower—we buy what we know.

Anyway, the mower has a special gear in it that you trip by pulling a little lever flush with the push bar. That makes it easier to push, making mowing a pleasure rather than a chore. Or so Hubby thought.

I told him when he bought the mower, he really should get the ride-on mower.

"Oh no, it will be a good way for me to keep fit. If I have a ride mower then it's too lazy."

I turned my mouth down in a disapproving grimace, "You're going to be sorry. I'll bet you buy a ride-on mower within 2 years."

He ignored me. The thing about staying married for a gazillion years is you have to learn when to ignore. Hubby is a master at it.

Well, it takes him about 6 hours to mow all the lawn we have. Even with the special gear to make things go easier, it's still a pretty big chore to mow front, back, sides.

We live in the country. The bad thing about living in the country

Rural Genius: Secrets to Long Term Marriages

is you get about 100% more weeds than you do in town. I mean there are weed seed just flying around looking for a good lawn to take rest and root.

So, often times mowing the lawn is really mowing the weeds down. Weeds grow faster than grass. I wonder why that is. Regardless, the 6 hours are often dedicated to mowing the many weeds down.

Hubby is pretty smart though, he splits it up over 2 days, 3 hours each day. You see, he can only mow until about 10 am and it's just too damned hot to continue. Even with a hat, you can get sunstroke here. This doesn't even count the over 80% humidity. The humidity, plus 100 degree F weather makes for an awfully high heat-index factor. Thus, any outside activity in the Summer is dedicated to the a.m. before the temperature hits 100F.

Well the third summer started up. Weeds were growing tall, and we were into the 3rd year of retirement. Hubby finally bought a ride-on mower. I delighted in reminding him that I predicted that he would one day buy one. He ignored my comment.

He bought a big yellow sucker that we nicknamed "Thor." Yes it was loud, like thunder and lightening—but we named it Thor because it could cut the grass in 1/2 hour. It could go around all the trees we have on the property with ease because it has a steering wheel and a very tight turning radius. It doesn't have two handles like a tank, it has a steering wheel—bummer.

How does it reduce the mowing time down to 1/2 hour from 6? Well, I'll tell you. I run the ride mower and hubby uses the push mower to get the little places that Thor misses. You see, since he

Hilda Carpenter

bought the ride mower, I go help him.

I mean, I have to stay in shape, too, right?

Hobbies

Retirement is a funny thing. Hubby and I worked for 40 years, taking only three, week-long vacations in all that time. Work defined us, drove us.

Well, plus we needed to pay for orthodontics, kids' sports, child care, private high school and college for the kids (and college for us—to get promoted we needed college degrees). Not to mention we needed to save for retirement, this simply meant that we needed to work like slaves to earn money. We were always the best employees we could be so we could get raises and promotions. I guess we were successful. We have some pretty great kids with straight teeth.

Weekends were filled with kids' activities, laundry, shopping and cleaning the house (I loved it when my kids were old enough to clean their own bathroom and do their own laundry—at 11 years old). We even taught the kids to cook at least one night a week, so we didn't have to. We gave the kids incentive to learn how to cook with a rule, "He who cooks does not have to clean up." Hubby taught them their favorite, Cheesey Weenies. Yep, it's about as bad as it sounds, and Hubby and I did the clean up while the kids flopped on the couch to watch TV, giggling about the great meal they had cooked.

Then, the kids went off to college, we continued working as slaves wishing for the day when we could retire. I planned on having pajama days and laze around reading. Maybe I'd go get coffee during the day with friends, start playing golf again.

But hubby? He had not visualized what he would do. This

Hilda Carpenter

worried me until one time my sister moved in with us. She had a bad break up of her marriage and needed a new start. She was going to stay for a couple of weeks that lasted over a year.

I love my sister, I do. But after you are both over 30, have had your own homes, living together can put a strain on that love.

Hubby was great though, he finally had someone who was a morning person (I'm not, never will be, don't even want to try). I was happy because sister and I were close again.

When she and I were not fighting.

About month nine of sister living with us, Steve said he wanted to go to a woodworking show that was in the downtown convention center. Wow, he had never even, I mean at all, expressed a desire to do woodworking. Sister declined the invitation to join us, so hubby and I braved the weekend traffic to head downtown.

I had no idea what to expect, but I am always up for an adventure.

We looked at planers, joiners, drill presses, lathes, sanders, band saws and more tools than I had ever seen.

We walked around the show several times and each time, hubby would stop at the demonstration of a lathe.

I finally said, "Does woodturning interest you?"

"I don't know."

It's so frustrating when he's wishy-washy. But to keep a long-term

Rural Genius: Secrets to Long Term Marriages

marriage there are times when you have to ignore the other person.

We walked around some more then ended up at the lathe demonstrator again. I said, "Buy it."

He looked over at me as if I had lost my little mind.

I stared at him, "If you don't buy it, I'm going to."

"What do you want with a lathe?" He sarcastically asked.

I sweetly answered, "A happy husband."

Well, I had no idea that to operate a lathe you needed all kinds of tools. So we bought the lathe and headed over to the "turning tools." Honestly, I never really knew there was a difference in woodturning and wood working. But I learn fast.

He had that sinking, overwhelmed look, I just handed them our credit card. We purchased (what I found out) was called a mini-lathe, a spindle gouge, roughing gouge, bowl gouge and some other things I simply could not identify.

Hubby was in heaven (if not feeling a bit remorseful about spending so much money). I said, "You needed a hobby."

He was off to the races after that. While sister and I swung between giggling, gossiping and fighting, hubby was in the garage making sawdust. Then he came in and presented a bowl!

It was really ugly, but I was so impressed.

Hilda Carpenter

Then he bought some more equipment and started turning pens, perfume canisters, more bowls and candle holders. They were really good. Sister would see the good stuff and claim, "Mine!"

About this time, we fully retired. I felt confident that Hubby had a hobby. Sister found a new place of her own to live. Life was good. While bragging on a recent pen that Hubby had turned to one of our friends, our friend said, "I didn't know you turned."

Hubby said, "I could only stand having 2 adult sisters in my home for so long before I needed to get out of the house. I don't smoke, drink, gamble or chase women, so this was it." He proudly held up a beautiful set of candle holders and smiled a knowing smile.

Thus, the birth of a hobby adds strength to marriages.

Rural Genius: Secrets to Long Term Marriages

Hobby as a Lifestyle

After Hubby and I retired, we decided that it was too expensive to stay where we lived. Well, Hubby decided it for us I should say.

We had a lot of changes at the same time. My sister, who lived with us over a year, had moved out. My daughter graduated college and came back to our home town. I had just finished my final degree and ready to put it to work.

Hubby had a hobby, I had work and friends.

Then, we moved from the big city in California to a red-neck, Bible-belt State. Red not blue State, oh dear.

Plus, we didn't even move to a city, we moved to the country. I mean the sticks. There's a road near our house that is in the middle of nowhere on the way to somewhere. It is really dark outside, because there is no light pollution. The good thing is there's absolutely no pollution of any kind, except when the Oak trees bloom.

I went insane, literally.

Hubby spent almost all his time out in the shop with his new big-boy lathe. I rattled around a house that is way to big for only 2 people.

Then, one day, I decided I needed to do something that would at least put me in the same room with Hubby, the only person I knew for 20 miles. Hell, just about the only person around for 20 miles.

Hilda Carpenter

So, I decided to learn how to carve wood. I mean at least I would be making chips while he made sawdust. He was getting really, really good at turning wood on his lathe. We started giving his pieces as Christmas presents. Me, I chipped away at a piece of bass wood and came out with a very strange looking car.

Unfortunately, my hands are not terribly strong, so carving was not fun at all.

So much for that hobby.

Hubby made all those beautiful pieces and made it look so easy. I decided that I needed to learn how to turn, too. The only problem was, hubby was always using his lathe and tools.

So, I started turning on the mini-lathe we bought him at an earlier point before retirement.

Now, the thing about hubby's turning is I never saw him at the beginning. I had no idea that pieces of wood could go flying off the lathe at light-speed. Well, I found out the hard way.

To understand turning wood, one has to understand that the wood needs to be held in what they call a chuck.

My problem was that I couldn't get the damned wood to stay in the chuck. I failed and failed and failed. Hubby would try to explain what I was doing wrong.

Well that went over like a lead balloon. You see in order to stay in a long-term marriage, it's always better if the spouse never, I mean never, tries to teach the other spouse how to do something.

Rural Genius: Secrets to Long Term Marriages

Hubby suggested that I take a class and join him at the local woodturner's club meeting.

I was hesitant to do this, since I didn't want to tread on his recently-found retirement independence. (It's easy for spouses to cling to each other during retirement—this leads to all kinds of problems, especially if you both have led very separate careers for 40 years).

But, it was either take the class, join the club, or never see hubby and go completely insane.

So, I took a class. I learned how to keep the wood in a chuck—sort of. But at least I got farther along than I had in trying to learn how to carve.

It was exciting when wood would go flying off in hubby's direction. It was exciting when he was turning raw wood and I would get showered by bark. In other words, we were a little to close (physically) to each other.

But, the good news was we could finally talk about common interests. I fell in love with the woodturning club because it was filled with little, old, retired men. My previous club experience had been with clubs that were mostly women. Women's clubs are scary because frankly in my experience, women are mean. Men are just funny.

There was a huge woodturning symposium happening about 3 hours from where we lived. We decided to go. I learned even more—and bought a lathe, a big-girl lathe. Since hubby didn't like for me to sharpen his tools, I bought my own tools.

Hilda Carpenter

Having a mutual hobby as a lifestyle is great in retirement. Hubby has become a professional woodturning artist. I have a lot of fun playing.

But the best part is that I'm no longer going crazy. Hubby didn't have to learn how to play golf (he thinks it's the most boring sport in the world), so he's happy.

And I get to get a smooch whenever I like it. Even though it does sometimes taste like sawdust, I just don't care!

Rural Genius: Secrets to Long Term Marriages

Escargot

My Hubby and I were great friends before we, er, became more than friends, about 2 years before we married.

When I met him, he was divorced and I was separated from Ex #2. Hubby had two kids and I had two kids. We had friends in common and we would all go to the beach, down to little sea towns, or to the park with all four kids. We had common friends and it was a safe situation for me, newly moved to California.

Now Hubby was nothing more than what we termed in the 80's, a "hunk." Meaning he was incredibly handsome, built, and smart to boot. He looked like the poster boy of a California man (you know like what the Beach Boys sang about?). In fact, he had even surfed during his youth on the southern California beaches.

I got pretty lonely anyway, and started feeling some "stirrings" toward this hunk of a man. But, we were "friends", nothing more.

Then one day he invited me and the kids to go with him and his kids to San Francisco. None of our other friends were able to make it on the trip with us. I have to admit, my little heart fluttered at the thought of just him and me (… and the kids) alone together in San Francisco. My imagination streamed forward thinking "I'll bet he takes me to a nice restaurant to eat!"

Saturday came, and he (…and his kids) came to get me and my kids. We all laughed and played games on the hour drive up to the City (In case you don't know, you are never to call San Francisco by the names "Frisco", "San Fran", etc. It's either San

Francisco or "The City". If you do make this fatal error, you're immediately dismissed by the locals as a buffoon).

We were headed to Fisherman's Wharf to play. Of course we were all starving by the time we located a parking place and unloaded all the kids.

As happenstance had it, there was a Burger King right there by the parking lot. Hubby says, "Hey, who wants Burger King?"

So much for a fancy dinner.

The day was still fun, and I was quite sure that the "friends only" deal was sealed. Then about 2 weeks later he asked me if I would like to go out to eat. I said, well the kids have already eaten, but if you come over, I'll make you a bologna sandwich.

He coughed and said, "Well, no I was wondering if you would like to go out to dinner with me—without the kids."

I didn't know what to say, the "friends only" status seemed at peril. Well, I didn't know what to say for about a nanosecond. The chance to go to dinner with the hunk to a place with cloth napkins, and didn't serve bologna was too much of a draw. "Yes, that sounds wonderful. Do you want me to meet you where and when?"

"Uh, no I'll come by and pick you up around 7 if that's ok."

Hmmm, maybe we're going to Burger King again, so to test it I said, "What should I wear?" The test of all women to see if: a) he knows about cultural norms; and b) if he's taking you someplace nice.

Rural Genius: Secrets to Long Term Marriages

"Oh wear things like you wear to work is fine." He sounded so confident. Sigh.

Now in California, business casual is like dressed up anyplace else in the country. So I was stoked. It meant (at that time), no jeans, hose, and show your legs! Wohoo!

So 7 pm that Saturday comes along and his daughter and son are with him. I wasn't worried, because he told me his daughter would babysit my kids. This was great, because my son had his son to play with and my daughter would be cared for by his daughter. Wasn't that considerate of him to take care of the baby sitting? I thought so myself. We say good bye to the kids.

We walked toward the car (the whole time I'm thinking, if this is a date, then he'll open my car door for me). He didn't.

So, I climb in the passenger side and say, "Where are we going?" all charming like. I actually was nervous.

He tells me the name of a restaurant that I didn't know.

Well, we get to a lovely, lovely restaurant with cloth napkins and everything!! Wohoo!

He asks me if I want to order any hors d'oeuvres. Wow dinner and a before meal snack—like REAL grownups!

I look at the menu and say, "Oh they have escargot!" I tell him I studied 5 years of French and they are a French delicacy (ok, I had to tell him then that I'd never been to France, but I knew it was a delicacy).

Hilda Carpenter

He turns to the waiter and says, "Escargot, please for the lady."

I'm a lady! This is looking up!

"You aren't having any?"

He says, "No I'll just have the main meal."

I smile (knowingly) and say, "You've never had them have you?" AHA! I get to show some sophistication here!! Yay me.

He smiles and says, "Well no, I haven't."

"Then how do you know you won't want it if you have never tried it?" I'm oh-so-charming with twinkling eyes.

I hoped I didn't bat the eyelashes too much.

The waiter brings the escargot with two little escargot forks.

I hand him one and take the other. "The best part is the garlic butter!" Oops may have shown my desert roots.

I pierce an escargot and charmingly hold it up for him to take off my fork.

He takes it into his mouth and swallows it immediately.

"You didn't chew it. Try another one."

This time he chewed it and I swear I could see it going down his throat as he raised his chin to help him swallow.

I said, "Ok, now you can say you've had escargot. Do you want more?"

"No thank you."

The evening went along wonderfully and we laughed and had a lot of fun. As we entered the car (still didn't open my car door) he snapped his seatbelt and held up the stolen little fork.

"For memories to come." I was hooked.

Slugs

After a few months of just being friends, Hubby and I decided to move in together to, ahem, save rent. Both of our current leases were ending. We rented a condo that would accommodate all the kids with an extra bedroom for him. Only he never moved into the extra bedroom, if you catch my drift.

It was a cool, two-story condo with separate covered parking behind. The front of the condo had a beautiful greenbelt area with curved walkways that were accented with flowers. I rarely saw anyone in the greenbelt area, but the area made you feel like there was a great expanse—not closed-in at all. I don't think I ever saw anyone going into their front doors, but it was pretty.

Behind the rows of condominiums, was a row of closed-garages. One garage aligned behind each condo. All the tenants would drive through an alley to get to their own garage. Once in the garage, we entered the patio through a door opposite of the big garage door.

The patio was a square area, probably 20x20 with bushes of lime trees, roses and other exotic plants surrounding the patio. The patio floor was laid with pavers. Opposite the garage was the sliding door to enter the condo. On each side of the patio were 7' fences that backed up the flora. We bought some cheap chairs and a little table so we could sit outside in the cool Northern California evenings. Unless your next door neighbors were loud, it felt like we were a million miles from civilization.

One evening we were sitting in the back patio with the sweet smell of the lime trees drifting over us. We were talking and

Rural Genius: Secrets to Long Term Marriages

laughing and looking up at the one star that was visible (there is a ton of light pollution). I told him how I missed seeing all the Texas Stars. That got us talking about where we grew up and the conversation comfortably drifted in and out.

Of course the main view was the garage wall, since our chairs didn't face the condominium. My eyes drifted to the wall and I saw this 4" long black thing. I said, "What in the heck is that?"

He said, "I don't know, what does it look like?"

I got up from my chair and walked over for a closer look. "It's black and yellow. It looks kind of wet. Well, it sort of looks like a huge snail, without a shell."

Now I grew up in the Chihuahuan desert of West Texas. We had snails, but they were probably about as long as the tip of your finger, and only came out after rain. But the distinguishing feature was their telescoping eyes.

"The thing has telescoping eyes like a snail! I've never seen anything like this in my life!"

He says, "Wow, go get some salt and pour on it to see what happens."

Well, him being a Californian boy, I figured he was in the know, so I ran through the sliding door and grabbed the salt from the kitchen.

I skipped over the pavers to the back wall and proceeded to throw salt on top of this strange creature.

At this point, I nearly threw up. The poor thing started writhing, oozing bubbles of yellow, and trying to escape the salt before it finally fell to its death.

"What in the HELL was that?" I screamed.

He started laughing his ass off.

"You KNEW what would happen!?" I yelled incredulously, I couldn't believe this best friend-now-lover would do something so mean to me, not to mention the snail without a shell.

He's still laughing, now falling out of his rickety, cheap chair.

The kids come out to see what all the commotion is. I tell them to get back inside, they are too young to see such destruction. Of course that command worked like refusing them donuts on Saturday morning. They ran past me and ooed and awed. Gag.

"OK smarty pants, what was that thing that I just killed."

He struggles not to laugh and says, "The Mascot of the University of Santa Cruz, CA."

I start tapping my foot, knowing that he is trying to extend the joke way beyond the fun part at this point. "Tell me what the HELL it is!" I demanded.

"A slug."

"A what?"

"Slug."

Rural Genius: Secrets to Long Term Marriages

My son says, "Oh yeah, I heard about these in school!"

My daughter wants to pick it up!

I usher the kids back into the house and tell them to go get ready for their baths.

"What the hell is a slug?" I feel so stupid.

"Well, it's sort of a — it's a — I guess you could say it's a snail without a shell." He sniggers.

I never ate another escargot again.

Hilda Carpenter

Birthday Present

While Hubby and I were living in sin at the townhouse with the slugs, we would often talk about our troubled childhoods. Actually, we didn't really have it all that bad, but we would entertain each other with the "who had it worst" tales.

Hubby came up with one about how his family had a motor home they would take on vacations into the southern California mountains. He had four sisters. I figured that gave him the edge on his childhood because I only had one younger sister, plus an older brother. Well, his story went on to say that he never got to sleep inside, and always had to sleep on the ground outside of the motor home, because there were not enough beds for everyone.

I told him that sounded actually pretty cool for a young boy to get to sleep out under the stars.

He reminded me of all the snakes, mosquitoes, scorpions and spiders that he had to fight off. Then he had to do latrine duty (their motor home didn't have a potty). Ick, ok that's pretty gross.

I said, well we never took vacations as a family. We were sharecropper farmer kids and during the summer it meant that we had to work either around the house or on the farm. I had no idea what a vacation was.

Well, that wasn't true exactly he reminded me. My grandparents sent all 5 of my cousins and me to special camps for 3 summers in a row.

I said, "That's not a family vacation—that was a vacation for

Rural Genius: Secrets to Long Term Marriages

mom and daddy."

But he had me, I did have a lot of fun at that camp.

Searching my mind, I finally came up with a story that would have beaten his beatific southern California beach experiences. I mean the guy looked like a Beach Boy, and had all the stories about surfing, having a dune buggy and in general a pretty good time.

"OK, I've got it. Remember in the 60's when Color TV first came to market?"

"Yes …" he wasn't quite sure where this was headed.

"Well, did you have a Color TV?" I sarcastically asked.

"Yeah, we did have a Color TV."

"OK, did you ever get to go to Disneyland?" Oh I was on a roll.

"Yes, mom would buy us a book of ride coupons. I would trade the A, B & C tickets for my little sisters' E tickets."

"What the Hell is an E ticket?"

So, he explained to me that back in the 50's and 60's the Disneyland rides were alpha coded. An "A" ticket was like the teacups. B was something like the merry-go-round carousel, etc. All the way up to the E ticket—that was Space Mountain! He further explained that there were far fewer E tickets in the coupon books than there were A-D.

Hilda Carpenter

Oh I so had him now.

"So, you had Color TV, and you got to go to the beach, AND you got to go to Disneyland. Poor you, you had to trade for the E tickets—thus getting fewer rides than your sisters, right?"

He puffed out his chest and said, "Yes, now isn't that sad?"

I took a sip of my wine and said, "Sit back little boy and I will tell you about a deprived childhood. We had to go to my grandparents house to see Color TV. That only happened a few times a year. Want to know what the most thrilling thing was about their Color TV?"

He chuckled at my dramatics and said, "What?"

"The NBC Peacock and the Wonderful World of Disney."

"The NBC Peacock? I mean I get the Wonderful World of Disney because the fireworks over Cinderella's castle were in color. But what's the deal with the Peacock."

"Well Mr. SoCAL — Grandmom would yell, 'The PEACOCK IS ON!! THE PEACOCK IS ON!' We would run as fast as we could so we wouldn't miss the beautiful peacock feathers as they opened. Now *that* was Color TV."

I continued by looking pitiful and saying, "So while you didn't even remember the colorful NBC Peacock ... and you got to see Disneyland fireworks in person, all we had was images on a box."

"OK, you win this round." He admitted.

Rural Genius: Secrets to Long Term Marriages

Well a few months later my birthday was coming up. He said he had a very special present for me.

I said, "Listen, no one ever remembers my birthday, much less with a present. Let's just take the kids out to Burger King and have a nice bottle of wine when we get back home."

Burger King was my signal that I really wanted to do something nicer, like get a babysitter and do something adult. He just smiled, and said, "OK."

My birthday is in August, the hottest month of the year anywhere in the northern hemisphere of the Earth. We were in the middle of a 7-year drought in California. I mean it was reminiscent of my life growing up around Pecos, a small Texas town located in the Chihuahuan Desert. My birthday this particular year fell on a Saturday and it had been an especially long week at work. On Friday (my birthday eve) I traversed the hour long commute home and could hardly wait to put on my t-shirt and flip-flops and have a big, no enormous glass of wine. Sit under the a/c and watch brainless TV. Maybe we'd order pizza delivery. I certainly didn't feel like cooking.

I parked my truck behind our townhouse and was surprised to see hubby working on his car. Now, his car was a Chevy, relatively new, and except for a few chocolate stains from a previous adventure, was pristine. I mean the thing ran like a top.

"What's wrong with your car?" I asked as I unloaded the kids and me into the hot garage.

"The damned alternator went out. I wasn't sure I was going to be able to start it when I left work. I got a jump off one of my buddy's car at work, but the battery is already dead again."

He had about the same length of commute as I did, so I sympathized with the dreaded-car-problem that always seems to happen to hard working people.

I said, "Well why don't you leave it for tomorrow? We'll get the parts you need to fix it at AutoZone, and you can get out of this heat right now. I mean, you can work on it early tomorrow when it's cool."

I wasn't in a very accommodating mood, I just wanted the flip-flops, braless t-shirt and wine. "I'll order some pizza."

Now when hubby gets focused, he becomes intense, and very hard headed. "No, I've got to fix it now."

He had that, I'm-pissed-and-I'm-going-to-take-it-out-on-the-world look that he gets. So, I just shook my head and herded the kids into the house.

After a bit, he came in slamming kitchen cabinets.

"What's wrong?"

"I've got to go back down to AutoZone because I don't have metric wrenches. I'm going to borrow your truck."

Metric wrenches? Well, I just stayed out of his way. But then he said, "Start packing."

Start packing? Start Packing? I didn't think I'd been that big of a bitch to him. What the FRICK was this about?

Rural Genius: Secrets to Long Term Marriages

He stormed out of the house, but I followed close on his heels. "What do you mean, start packing?"

"We're going to get out of here as soon as I fix this damned car."

Whew at least he said "we."

I ventured a timid question —

"Where are we going?"

His mouth was a slice (his lips get really thin when he's pissed) and said, "Disneyland."

Huh?

"What do you mean, Disneyland?"

"I'm giving you a trip to Disneyland for your birthday. It was going to be a surprise, but the damned car is broken and I have to fix it before we can get on the road."

"The kids, too?" I was still not believing my ears.

"Well, of course." He huffed.

I was dumfounded—not only did he remember my birthday, but he was going to give me Disneyland as a present. Tears welled up in my eyes and I said, "That's the nicest almost-present I ever had."

His shoulders slumped and he muttered, "It was going to be a surprise. I was going to act like we were going out to dinner and a hotel, then I was going to drive us all down to LA tonight." He shook his head. Beaten by a Chevy …

"I don't need Disneyland today. We can go another time. Just the thought that you were going to that much trouble for me is present enough. Come on, let's change and relax."

"No, I'm giving you Disneyland. If you will go pack up yourself and the kids, I'll be ready to go in an hour, come Hell or High Water."

The story ends with me, my son in his Mickey-Mouse ears, my daughter asleep in her stroller, and hubby's arm around me at the end of a long Saturday watching the fireworks over Cinderella's castle.

I have the most wonderful Hubby in the world—he gave me and my kids Disneyland—in person.

I didn't even think about the NBC Peacock ever again until I told this story.

Sigh, I love that man.

Rural Genius: Secrets to Long Term Marriages

Broken Legs

Hubby and I had been married about 9 or 10 years, when he really became an expert at snow skiing. I mean the man was wickedly awesome on the hardest slopes. We would often pack up the kids and trek up to Tahoe to one of the skiing resorts and stay in a cheap motel. The way we saw it was why spend money on a hotel, when we could spend it on lift tickets. We were in accord on this point. The only complainers were the kids, because we all slept in the same room and Hubby, well, he snored like a freight train. Poor kids.

About this time, Hubby went to work for a National Lab that was an hour closer to the slopes than where we lived. Yes, he had an hour-long commute every day, each way. The various employees at the Lab would often schedule a ski day. This meant they would all meet at the lab early in the morning, then pack up into one or two cars and head to the closest ski resort for a day of skiing. Hubby would return back to our home around 10-midnight.

I had a suspicion that he might be having an affair with one or two women at the lab. Why did I suspect this? Well, one of them invited us to her house and she couldn't take her eyes off of him. Yeah, that's a pretty good clue that a woman is scheming on your man, or vice versa. Now to Hubby's credit, I didn't really see him scheming on to either of the two lady friends, at least while he was around me. But each invitation to have couples get together it became more and more apparent that one of these ladies, in particular, was quite smitten with my Hubby. She had beautiful, natural, red hair, of course.

Unfortunately at the time, Hubby and I were having tons of

problems in our marriage. The causes? Well mix an angry teenager with alcohol, two hard work schedules—and voila, you have marital problems. The only problem we really didn't have in our marriage was money. Hubby and I were quite compatible when it came to money. Probably if one of us gambled or was a shop-a-holic, that would have put the death knell on our marriage.

So, the little redhead who was interested in Hubby most likely picked up the testy-vibes that Hubby and I were sharing in those days. Women are like that, they can "smell" bait in the water. Hubby was most definitely bait in the water as far as she was concerned. I couldn't really blame her, frankly I was pretty sick of him, and him of me. Well, that and the fact that he was a hunk.

Well, Hubby decided to take a vacation day and go up with the work buddies (including the redhead). They "all" planned to ski Friday, spend the night at a hotel, then take Saturday to ski. Thus, he would be home Saturday night. I was suspicious, no that's not right, I pretty-well figured that there would be alcohol and some room shifting if the redhead had her way about it.

Ce la vie, I'd been there done that, and like I say, I had problems of my own with the teenager and Hubby wasn't helping out with that at all. In fact, he was making it a lot worse by picking fights with the teen, when he was actually mad at me.

In other words, I was ready to let him go.

Then, about 6 pm Friday night I get a call from the redhead. What the hell was this? She let me know that hubby had broken his leg and they were going to drive him down to our city from Tahoe, could I please meet her at the hospital?

Rural Genius: Secrets to Long Term Marriages

I paused, then said, "Wait —Run that one by me again—He broke his leg—You are driving down the mountain with him, 300 miles from the slope to the hospital here? And you want me to meet you at the hospital?"

"Yes, that's right."

Well what could I say? I agreed to meet her.

For some ungodly reason I was really pissed at him and worried at the same time. I cannot tell you if I was pissed because he broke his leg, or my imagination of him having the affair that night was wrong. I know, it makes no sense, but women often don't make any logical sense.

I called a couple of friends of mine to stay with my teens, then drove to the hospital in time to meet our car, with the redhead driving it. Hubby was in the cargo area, facing backward with his leg touching the back panel of the jeep. The redhead's friend (the other one I thought was scheming on Hubby) was waiting by her own car.

I asked both of them, "What happened?"

"He broke his leg, the ski patrol took him to the First Aid station. The doctor there said that he had a really, really bad break and if we took him to a local Tahoe hospital, you would have to come up there. We figured you would want him to be local."

"You mean he's been in pain all this time?" I wanted to be pissed at these ladies, I really did, but I was finding it hard to hold anger toward them. I mean they drove 120 miles out of their way to bring hubby to me.

Hilda Carpenter

"Oh no, they gave him pain meds to make it down here." They seemed genuinely worried and sincere.

Concurrently while talking to the ladies, the medics at the hospital came out to get Hubby. They had a wheel chair. The ladies stopped talking to me long enough to say, "You're going to need a gurney. He can't get into a wheel chair."

Well how the hell did they know that, I thought to myself. Wasn't it the wife's place to order RNs around? Humph.

Then, the medic started lifting hubby out the back of the jeep. There he was smiling ear-to-ear. "They gave me really good drugs."

Obviously.

The medic jerked hubby forward to take him out of the back of the jeep and the most piercing cry I have ever heard (including colic-babies) emanated from the jeep.

"I think I'll get a gurney." Well brilliant. That's what the redhead said . . .

The redhead touched my arm, and said, "Let us know how he does." The meaningful look of love and concern was plastered all over her face. It was then that I knew to the bottom of my heart that she loved my Hubby. And it was then, that I knew I would never, never give him up.

When you get married, part of the vows often exchanged says, "In sickness and in health."

Rural Genius: Secrets to Long Term Marriages

This was my first experience of real, live sickness. Wa-ay more than the flu or kidney stones.

The RN and medic managed to get hubby on the gurney, and the emergency room doctor came out to help.

Well the doctor managed to get behind hubby while the medics and RNs kept his leg straight. I couldn't help but notice that his foot was perpendicular to the forward shaft of the leg (that was encased in a temporary cast). Ugh, I really wanted to be sick, but kept hearing our minister's voice saying "in sickness and in health." This was definitely one of those sickness times.

After getting him on a table, they took a portable X-ray of his leg. The emergency room doctor showed me the X-ray.

"Holy SHIT!" I yelled and woke up some drunk who was sitting in ER. "He has multiple knees, and the bone looks like it's a big oak tree." There was not one straight bone in his lower leg.

The doctor looked at me and said in an Asian accent, "Belly bad, belly, belly bad. We need to call orthopedic surgeon." Well it was belly bad. He was right.

I went in to stand beside the hospital bed as the nurses were trying to pull off his sock! I could see the leg elongate as they pulled on his foot without budging the sock. I mean socks are intended to stretch . . . Legs and ankles aren't! I screamed about as loud as hubby did and said, "CUT OFF THE DAMNED SOCK! STOP PULLING ON IT!!"

The nurses ignored me until the doctor came in and calmly said,

"Cut off." Thankfully they pulled out those weird scissors and chopped off his sock and clothes.

I was thinking, "Can you please get him some more pain medicine? If not for him for me." But I didn't interfere again. By this time the RN is pretty pissed at me for making her look bad in front of the doctor, so it took a while before the morphine came. Damnable woman. I know her night must have been pretty bad —But shit, she had not seen the Xray, I had!!

I hold hubby's hand and said, "I'll be right here, my love. My hunk."

He turned his head to me and looked at me with the eyes of a totally drugged out person and said, "The snow was absolutely awesome!"

I started laugh/crying. The next day, he had a 4 hour surgery. That's when we found out he has some weird allergy called malignant hypothermia. Now this condition is bad, really bad. It's an allergic reaction to gas anesthesia. His temperature got up to 107 degrees F. Everyone was worried he was going to die.

"DIE?" Oh shit, this is bad. Belly belly bad. Why was I worried about some bimbo he worked with? I chastised myself for all the mean thoughts I had had.

Well, he didn't die. After about a week in the hospital, he came home and lived in a hospital bed in the family room, because he couldn't make it up the steps. Every two hours I had to come down to empty his pee jar. This is when "in sickness and health" really kicks in. I mean it's one thing to wake up every two hours to give him pain medicine. But to have to empty the pee jar when

Rural Genius: Secrets to Long Term Marriages

you're half asleep is just, uh, rude. I didn't mind bathing him, or carrying the poop pan, because that happened during the day, but that nighttime pee jar, ugh.

After about 3 months, the doctor gave him the ok to start physical therapy, which included using crutches.

Now was the time, Hubby was going to be tested with the "in sickness and in health" vow… I took away his pee jar. Yep, that's me, the meanie who took away the pee jar. I knew if he had to pee bad enough he would get out of the hospital bed and exercise. "The path to healing is not laying down." I told him. He was more than a little pissed (sic) at me. But my approach worked.

The vow sickness/health to me means getting him through the malignant hypothermia, and not giving him up to another woman when our relationship is sick.

The phrase, to him means, putting up with me when I take away his pee jar.

Hilda Carpenter

Trust Builds from Trustworthiness

OK, I admit it. I spent most of my adolescence and young adult life as a jealous fiend who didn't trust anyone. I mean anyone. I figured that Ex #1 and Ex #2 were cheating on me all the time. In fairness to me, it didn't help when Ex #1 came home drunk from a party with his friends that included some pretty hot women and I wasn't invited. Or when I walked into Ex #2's office and one of his smoking-hot workers was sitting vixon-like on the arm of his office chair cradling his shoulders with her arm.

Of course, I was smarter than they were. When I cheated on someone else, I was very, very sneaky. They were always blown away by the time I let them know I was done with them and on to someone else (literally). Thus, I discovered not to trust anyone, much less myself.

When I finally agreed to marry Hubby, my Dad wrote a letter to my most precious aunt saying, "Well she's gone and gotten married again! It reminds me of Uncle Frank, you know? Remember when he married #8 at 80?" My Daddy went on to write, "One time I asked Uncle Frank why he kept getting married. Uncle Frank answered, I need a woman in my life and they always find out my extracurricular activities."

There you have it, It's in my damned DNA. Dad was a philanderer as well. Gossip in a small town always seeks the people that it can most hurt. My mom was stoic and meaner than Hell to him. It was a vicious cycle between the two of them, until finally they split up after 25 years of marriage.

So exchanging vows with hubby, I thought about Uncle Frank.

Rural Genius: Secrets to Long Term Marriages

Did I really want to have the same life that he, my Dad and my Mom had? Did I want to live always looking over my shoulder for either the redhead that was after my husband, or the next man in my life?

No, I guess I didn't. Because as I said those vows to Hubby, my Grandmother's words rang in my ear: "To trust you have to be trustworthy."

I'll admit at the time she gave me those words, I really didn't get it. I thought she was saying that my partner had to be trustworthy in order for me to trust the son-of-a-bitch. But as I stood there in front of the Preacher, with my children witnessing these vows. The clarity of the meaning came to my soul. I was the one who had to be trustworthy! If I trusted myself to behave morally, then I could trust the other person.

It was so simple. I wanted to tell Grandmom thank you, but she was already too old to travel to my wedding. So with hubby's entire family, and my children witnessing our vows, I said, "To Honor and Cherish" which in my head was the same thing as being worthy of his trust.

Now, there have been times, I'm not going to kid you, that keeping trustworthiness is not so simple. But I can say that over these nearly 30 years, I am trustworthy more than not.

Ok, I still get a little jealous of redheads, except for my redheaded step-daughter and granddaughter! Hubby really is quite a hunk and does catch the eyes of the ladies.

The good news is he only has eyes for me, bless him.

Hilda Carpenter

"Success is walking from failure to failure with no loss of enthusiasm." —Winston Churchill

When newlyweds honor couples with marriage longevity at the reception dance, typically the DJ or conductor announces over a loud speaker for those with 5 or less years of marriage to take their seats. Then he progresses in 5-year increments until the last couple dancing has the longest years of marriage to the same person. It's a lovely ceremony, honoring those who have chosen to take the chance that their relationship will outlive the statistics that say 50% of marriages fail.

Then, when the oldie-goldies remain, they have usually been married over 50 to 60 contiguous years to the same person. Now, that is a long time. Think about it. Most wars don't last longer than 5-20 years, unless it's in the MidEast, because those tribal wars have gone on for centuries.

Warlords aside, how is it that these old farts managed to stick together for so long. Much less, if they are still smiling at one another. Well, Hell, think about it, they WERE dancing together, so that implies that they can actually touch each other, coordinate their movements to music for as long as it takes to weed out the other couples with less matrimonial longevity.

When the last couple remains on the dance floor with the newly weds, the announcer asks the all-important question: "What do you feel is the key to long-term marriage?"

The answer never includes: "He was lost on a remote island for 60 years and only returned last year. No one else would have me, so I never declared him dead, and I never divorced him due to abandonment."

Nope, no one answers that way. I've been to many, many weddings where someone facilitates this longevity exercise. The answers I've heard? "Humor." "She's always right." "Don't go to bed angry." "Always work together on the big problems." "Have kids." "Don't have kids." "Always tell her she's the best cook." "Always tell him you appreciate how hard he works." "Tell her she's the best mother." "Tell her/him you love him/her every day."

I never hear things like, "Lie to him/her." "Have multiple affairs." "Keep your mouth closed even when he/she is being an idiot." "Put up with him/her." "Kick him in the nuts/Kick her in the crotch." "Throttle him/her on regular schedule." "Surprise him/her with a bat in the face." "Burn his dinner." "Quit your highly successful job and ask her to move into a yurt." "Be sure to join the country club." "Play lots and lots of golf." "Play lots and lots of bridge." "Never play cards together." "Spend everything you have and go insanely in debt without any prospect of ever getting out of debt without cheating your vendors out of their hard-earned money." "Buy a bigger house." "Buy an even bigger house." "Make slaves out of your kids." "Work into the evening so you can miss all the homework drama." "Tell him he is boring you to tears and you will most likely pull out your eyes if you have to listen to him one —More—Minute!"

No, the longevity folks try to pick the one gem that will hold the couple in marital bliss for as many years as they have been.

Herein lies the myth—That there are blissful marriages every second, every minute, every hour, every day of the years.

Hilda Carpenter

However, if we look at Winston Churchill's infamous quote and apply it to the institution of marriage, therein lies an amazing concept. Marriage is full of failures. But if you can keep the enthusiasm even through those failures, most likely you will be at someone's marriage doing this wedding dance and answering the mystical question for some newly-married couple.

My grandparents, both maternal and fraternal, were married over 50 years. They loved each other, sure, but there were times when they absolutely hated the other person with a passion as strong as the love they shared that led them to marry in the first place. My great-grandparents were married over 60 years—Same story.

These six couples knew that marriage longevity is found in the dark moments in relationships. Those times that seem as if they will go on forever. He's unfaithful, she's unfaithful with someone else.

He doesn't show affection/She is frigid. These two most likely exist at the same time.

The man or woman who is taken by surprise that the other has been unfaithful, or is thinking about being unfaithful is simply unrealistic and doesn't pay attention to the failures that have happened along the way.

If you pay attention to the failures, you find a roadmap to marital longevity.

I remember once after Hubby and I had separated for over a year, we reunited and moved back in together. I was reticent to have confidence that we had reconciled beyond any fear that our marriage might fail. For Hubby all the old hurts were simply in the past and no longer were applicable to our marriage.

I remember looking in to Hubby's crystalline blue eyes and saying, "We are so different in the way we think, the way we approach problem-solving, raising children, that the only way I can agree to reconciliation is if I have your promise that we will both work at this marriage every second, minute, hour of every day."

His expression betrayed the anger he felt, the frustration of having to jump through yet, another hurdle I was throwing out at him. Then his face calmed, he looked at me in earnest and said, "I can do that."

I said, "Me too."

It was only a month later that we were sharing breakfast at one of our favorite cafes. We were chatting and laughing, then suddenly all I could see was red. I was absolutely, with the utmost purity of hate, simply furious at him. I was so furious that I couldn't even listen to what he was saying as the conversation continued.

I observed myself "acting" as if I was pleasantly listening to his banal talk, while I observed my complete dissociation from the conversation.

Thankfully, I stopped him from talking by saying, "I need to interrupt you."

His face again betrayed his frustration of my right-angle shift in the conversation, taking him off track of our seemingly pleasant conversation.

I looked at him with pure honesty in my face and heart and said, "I am so furious at you that I cannot even hear what you are saying. I think this is one of those moments where we have to slow things down to seconds in time to dissect what is going on here."

He placed his palms on the table and said, "OK, how do we do this?" He was no longer irritated, just curious to help me get to what had made me so incredibly angry.

I paused (a new behavior in me) and said, "It would help me if we could reconstruct this conversation."

He seemed pleased to know that I had an idea of how to get to my anger, rather than calling him an insensitive prick like I usually did.

"OK, you were talking about ——— (topic doesn't really matter for the retelling of this story)."

He said, "Yes, I said ——— (again response is irrelevant for the retelling of this story)."

I said, "No, that didn't make me angry."

He patiently stepped the conversation back phrase by phrase as I answered, "No that didn't make me mad."

Then he said, "Then I asked you what you thought about ——————— (again, topic is irrelevant)."

I excitedly pointed my finger at his face and exclaimed, "THAT'S

Rural Genius: Secrets to Long Term Marriages

IT!! You asked me my opinion about something, then you told me I was wrong."

I sucked in air as if I had been underwater for too long and said, "How can my OPINION be wrong?? It's MY opinion!!! I can have an opinion and to me it isn't wrong. No one has the right to tell me my opinion is wrong, it's mine as sure as my eyes are teal."

He sat back in his seat, sucking in the same refreshing air, "Oh I'm sorry. That's not what I meant to say, I meant to say, I disagree with your opinion."

The tension between us evaporated as I smiled and said, "I have no problem with you disagreeing with my opinion. Just don't tell me my opinion is wrong."

A simple failure in communication—But we approached each other with an attitude of enthusiasm for the relationship. My respect for him exponentially grew, as did my respect for myself.

Success is walking from failure (in communication) to failure (in life) with no loss of enthusiasm.

If one day sweet Hubby and I are dancing to a wedding song, and we are asked our opinion of a long-term marriage secret. I hope I will remember Churchill's quote.

Magic Wand for Change

When I was a young lass, like many other women, I thought if I got a man who had the basic building blocks for a good partner, I could shape the rough spots of him to be my perfect man.

I find that most people truly believe this. I don't any more. At all. I mean all it takes is a couple of divorces and a third marriage to finally "get" that you just don't have a Magic Wand that will change the other person's behavior. Oh, change does occur after about 30 years, but it is painfully slow and waiting for a pot of water to boil, change won't happen if you are watching it, much less expecting it.

By expecting any change in another person, I set myself up for extreme resentments. I would say things like, "You KNOW I want you to—(fill in the blank)." Or I might be even more lovely by saying, "I TOLD YOU I hate it when you treat me like that."

When I gave those kind of clues to the partner, what I finally figured out was it gave them ammo to use against me the next time they were irritated with me. Well, color me stupid, I am a slow learner on this one to say the least.

Then, each day, the resentments grow greater and greater and GREATER, until I absolutely hate the air around him, and would love to kill him if I weren't so afraid of prison.

I decided to make a big change for myself once upon a time. I decided to try sobriety so that I could make some sense out of myself and my life. So, for 14 years nary a tiny drop of alcohol passed my lips. I even went to AA for a while. I entered into long-term therapy. What I learned there was I needed to set a moral compass for myself. Second, I learned that if I expected the world to cater to me, then I would be disappointed every time. Third, I learned that using alcohol to get out of being in a relationship—meaning attuning to that relationship—spells disaster in every occasion. Relationships require a lot of attention. More than I had ever realized I needed to put in.

My sponsor liked the little sayings of AA: "Expectations are nothing more than premeditated resentments." She also liked the one that said, "My stinkin' thinkin' got me here." Now, that one I still have a bit of trouble with, I think I have trouble with it because it implies that I was never supposed to think, grow, learn from my mistakes. But she liked it a lot. Her point was that I needed a committee to help me make decisions, until I could finally make clear choices that served me, unselfishly. I know, that didn't make sense to me either at first. But, if I am always looking to how I can be a better person in the world, then every decision I make really is unselfish.

After about 14 years in the AA program, I stepped out. I had learned what I needed to learn. I was able to disentangle from destructive relationships without secretively sabotaging myself or them. This learning has helped a whole lot where in-laws are concerned. It has helped me say, "Lord, save me from my anger, this is a sick person. Your will not mine be done."

Now, I'm not a religious freak, but when I really get angry at someone, or at myself, it helps to detach from the situation and realize I really am not in charge, I don't have a magic wand that can change me, or someone else.

Let me take another tact. If, like Cinderella's fairy godmother, I have a magic wand that can create a fantastical situation for a person (even if that person is me), how wonderful that sounds. However, the fairy godmother's admonition, "The magic will end." always comes true: Midnight, can and will always come.

If I have fairy godmother's wand and can change the other person into something I want, then I will be angry when they do not change. The trick is figuring out who has the magic wand thinking — Me or him? It doesn't really matter, I finally learned to be comfortable being me. If you make enough relationship mistakes, that lesson will come through. I got smarter about my choices and I know *how* to be, not *who* to be.

I watch other peoples' behaviors to see *how* they behave, not who they want to be. It works.

Take Hubby, he can be a royal pain in the ass. He can also be the kindest, most thoughtful person I believe I have ever known. He can tease me to the point of distraction, and he can comfort me when I ask for comforting.

So I gave my magic wand back to the fantastical fairy godmother. Marriages and committed relationships are for grownups—no room for magic.

Rural Genius: Secrets to Long Term Marriages

Lying

When I made the vows to Ex #1 and #2 and even to Hubby, I don't really think I was lying. But then again, the Catholics believe you can lie through omission. Hmm, well, are you lying if you don't even know you are lying? Then I find out later that what I said was a big fat lie? For example, the three special words, "I love you." How can those be a lie? Well they are, trust me. I did mean them at the time I said them, but then again — If you have your one and true love that you are going to say "I do" to, you're supposed to say you love them.

Now in the case of Ex #1, I said I love you because I was desperate for him to love me. Yep, that would fall into the category of lying. I never *said* I was desperate, now did I? As far as Ex #2, I again said "I love you." But good grief I had met him 3 weeks before we got married. I guarantee those people who believe in fast engagements (hell we really didn't have an engagement, come to think of it) are truly putting a lot of money on the black 13 at the Roulette table. There is absolutely no way that you meet someone, and know whether you love them within a three WEEK period! Good grief.

Armed with all my failures, I believe I still lied to hubby the first time I said "I love you" to him. I waited a long time before I said it. We'd already bedded each other, and I didn't say it. It wasn't until almost a year into our relationship that I admitted I loved him. So, what was that? Desperation? No, because I had a pretty good paying job and he and I were splitting the rent by that time, so I didn't marry him for security, nor did I say I love you to make him feel secure—

Well, hmm is that true?

I think I probably said "I love you" to make him know that I wasn't going to cheat on him like his ex did.

As a marriage continues toward that fateful 7 year mark, (I do believe there is such a thing as a 7-year itch) what happens is that habit forces us to lie to each other. For example, let's say a couple says, "I love you." Every day at the breakfast table, or at night before dropping off to sleep. Is it said with the same reverence that it was said at the very beginning of the relationship? Or, is it said because to not say it feels weird. For me, not to say it just felt weird. I mean I put my shoes on the same way every day, right foot gets shod before the left foot. It's a habit.

I once read one of those inspirational books to help you become more consciously aware, and the book recommend that I switch the order of putting my shoes on, e.g., put the left one on first in this case. It felt weird. Did I feel more consciously aware? Nah, not really. To be perfectly honest I hadn't ever thought about the shoe order before then. Did knowing that I put my right foot forward first help me achieve a higher order of consciousness? Of course not. I promptly forgot it as soon as the shoes were on and I was headed out to work. Another suggestion was to wash my hands opposite, e.g., if my right hand covers my left hand when I was, then flip it. Good grief.

There is such a concept of mindfulness that I very much agree with. I wish I had practiced mindfulness more carefully when I chose my words. Or realized that just because my partner doesn't tell me he loves me, it doesn't mean he hates me, or is ignoring me. Maybe he's just happens to be thinking about which order he puts his shoes on.

If I think about the failures in my marriages, there were a lot of things that went wrong. In the case of Hubby, when we separated, I truly, truly could have easily taken a golf club (9 iron of course) and bashed his head in. I was hurt, angry, and I sure as hell should not have said, "I love you" as he walked out the door. I'm sure he wanted to borrow my 9 iron about that time. Lying bitch!

The reason I said I loved you as he was walking out of the door was because I really somewhere within me knew I loved him. I just didn't like him very much at that moment. He didn't really like me either, although he probably was nicer than I was. Nah, he's always nicer than I am. It's infuriating sometimes.

When my marriages went off track and I "mindfully" re-examined what went wrong, it all started with a lie. Maybe it was a lie of omission, maybe it was a bald face lie (I'll be home by 6, then I arrive at 8 pm). I could kid myself and have an inward dialogue that would blame him for being angry at me for being late. Didn't he KNOW how important I was? Good grief, again.

So, the lie in being late and the internal dialogue, is that I didn't take the time to say why I didn't want to come home. I didn't say that my job was overwhelming. I didn't say, I just wanted to get home after the kids were fed, because I didn't feel like cooking tonight.

No, those internal dialogues are the most dangerous lies of all. They are the most dangerous because for me, it meant I was not communicating with my partner. It meant that taking the time to nurture the relationship was more effort than I wanted to give.

Thus, introduce the concept of the "wedge". If you look at a wedge as an angle with the X & Y points on 0, that means that you are totally on the same page with your partner. However, if I kept my internal dialogue to myself, I moved right of 0 (me being X) and he moved up or down from the point of 0 on the Y axis. Each time we didn't "work" on the relationship it was a matter of widening that wedge. The sad part is that the simplicity of the wedge metaphor is invisible to both parties.

After Hubby and I had been separated for over a year, he came over to the house and told me that it was time for him to move on. That if we didn't have hope of reconciling in my mind, that he could not live in limbo anymore, he needed to hire a lawyer. Honestly, I was heartbroken. I held my sorrow in check (no internal dialogue, just silence) and I said to him, "If that is what you need to do for your own happiness. I understand. I cannot say at this point that we do or don't have a chance of reconciliation. I'm still trying to figure out how we work together to make our marriage work, with teenagers." Then I told him, "I don't have anyone waiting in the wings to move in as soon as you are gone." Now this was clearly new behavior for me not to have a reserve parachute into another relationship, but it was absolutely the truth.

Then, I looked at him with my teal-blue eyes that were filled with tears and said, "I do know that I love you with all of my heart and soul. I just don't know how to fix this."

He gazed at me, the sunshine sparkling off his blond hair, and said, "OK. I'll wait for you." He meant it.

Our wedge had reset to 0,0. We were on the same page.

Within a month he moved home, to my utter delight and absolute terror! Delight that we had reset the wedge between us to zero, and terror of going through the pain of separating again if we were wrong, if we weren't strong enough to keep the points at 0,0.

It all worked, and the sex that night blew the roof off. Of course I had been going over to his apartment for booty calls the entire year we were separated, so I can honestly say that I never had to fake anything with this wonderful Hubby of mine.

About a year later, we were taking time out to work on any creeping wedges that might be coming up. I asked him, "When

Rural Genius: Secrets to Long Term Marriages

you said that you were going to have to hire an attorney that afternoon, what kept you from doing that?"

He told me an absolute truth, "I was testing you. I didn't want to divorce, but I had to find out what was in your head."

Ok, he lied at that point in time, but it was a good lie, because he was seeking information. That is probably the only time I can think of in our marriage that a lie totally worked for us. My answer gave him the strength to keep hoping. To keep loving me, to not give up on us.

So, there are times when a lie is absolutely necessary. "Do these pants make my butt look big?" Is a good time to lie to her. "Have you ever had a better lover than me?" Good time to lie to him.

Otherwise keep the dialogue out of the internal and on the table to beat off the wedge monsters.

Hilda Carpenter

A Hubby Who Remakes Himself

Hubby grew up fast. He married young and went to work in the emerging computer industry in southern California. It was a good industry to be in and soon he was known as an expert data processing employee. He and his ex had two beautiful children, so his road was pretty well paved that he would remain in an industry that paid pretty well. He could provide and protect his family.

Men have a mission in life that has been ingrained in to their DNA since caveman days. In caveman language it was "Ugh, me go get food. You stay in cave—it safer." So caveman would venture out into the wilds to risk life and limb to bring back some tasty meat for the cavewoman to cook.

When a person gets a divorce, there are weird little things that they keep. These items have sentimental value for that one person. In hubby's case after we moved in together, I discovered he had this cheap-ass little trivet. It wasn't a porcelain tile, it was cardboard, with a sepia-toned picture of a bunch of birds. I decided it was doomed to be discarded when we started the process of combining kitchens. Ooo big mistake. He grabbed it out of the trash can and cleaned it off, lovingly placing it in one of the kitchen drawers.

What on earth was that about? I didn't say anything at the time, but later after he was asleep, I went into the kitchen and pulled the trivet out of the drawer. The picture was of a covey of quail. The daddy quail looked out above the reeds, as momma quail held her wings over her chicks. The trivet had a pithy saying, "The cares of a family."

It took me years to really understand what that trivet meant. One evening I pulled it out and put a big pot of beans on top of it. I mean after all, it was a trivet, right? Hubby grabbed the pot and replaced the trivet with a hot pad. "I don't want the pot to burn it!"

At that time, I really looked at the trivet and tried to understand its deeper meaning. When I thought about how protective hubby was, and what a reliable provider he was, I thought about the cave man and woman. Hubby had his well-defined role in life. Nothing could change that. He was the Quail Cock. I was the Quail Hen.

Years went by, our kids grew up and left our nest. Hubby still saw himself as the provider and protector, but he became confused and depressed about his role. His Quail Hen (me) was very independent and made sufficient money that she didn't depend on his salary. His children no longer needed his wisdom (if you've had kids you know that they go through about 20 years where they think they don't need your wisdom). So, he began to question what his meaning in life was.

Then the fateful day came when he lost his job. He was too old to compete with the younger, cheaper labor force. He was truly devastated and sought to figure out his life's mission. Well, he sought, and sought and sought—and made me completely crazy.

I guess you could say this Quail Hen became the Quail Cock's muse. I asked Hubby about the occasions in his life where he lost track of time because he was doing something he really liked to do. He could not name anything at anytime in his life. Such was his depression and grief.

Finally, I understood. Hubby needed an outlet for all the pent-up talent that the computer industry didn't need.

One day, we decided to go to a wood working show, just because we didn't have anything else to do—and frankly I needed to get out of the house, because as I said, he was mopey and making me crazy.

So, we brought home a lathe, some steel tools, and some wood. It's been 16 years since that time, people from all over the country buy his beautiful art.

I smile at that quail trivet now with deep fondness. It represents to me the wonderful character of this man who could remake himself from protector and provider to artist.

Not many people can remake themselves into something completely different, especially in mid-life, and still maintain the strength of character, but Hubby has. He often says, "I had no idea that I had an artistic bone in my body, I was too busy making a living for money, not nurturing my soul. I'm proud of my family and the sacrifices I made to take care of them. But, I love my life now. If my Quail Hen had not kicked me in the ass, I'd still be lost looking for the same path, the wrong path."

God I love him. And I'll never get rid of that trivet. Because he still protects us, just by being happy.

Part 2 Blended Families—Kids and Family are Hard on a Marriage

Hilda Carpenter

Family is Hard on a Marriage

You can have the most perfect relationship with another person that has little or no problems, until you are around his parents/family or your parents/family. I call this the relationship-disturbance dynamic (RDD). If you are both orphans, this dynamic might be seen with your friends. If you have children the RDD exponentially increases and will last for the next two decades. If you are divorced with kids and marry another person (especially if he or she has children) the RDD moves into the complexity of problems like quantum physics.

In other words, if you and your partner never expose yourself to any social circle, you'll probably just have to deal with the relationship-disturbance dynamic when one of you is in a bad mood, or has a habit that drives you crazy.

These next few stories comically demonstrate how the RDD occurred for me. Now keep in mind, I had two failed marriages before this one. I had one child from each of my first two marriages—and the marriage broke up within 1-2 years after having the child. I merged my 2 kids with Hubby's 2 kids and with a lot of gray hairs and wrinkles later, we are now grandparents together.

A lot of people ask me the reason for Hubby and my success, I tell them we held on tight and fought like Hell.

They usually walk away with a strange look on their face. I mean how do I relate 30 years of marriage in a one-sentence answer? I still can't think of a better way to describe it than: "Hold on tight and fight like Hell."

Hilda Carpenter

Fish Scales

One time my Ex #1 and I wanted to go fishing. We decided to tag along with my parents. Daddy had a camper and his family had a ranch with stocked water tanks. The fish were really biting and we had a huge mess ready to clean and fry by the end of the first day.

In my family, the women are allowed to fish, but don't have to clean the fish. The messy, dirty work of scaling and gutting the fish goes to the men, and the women cook the fish. I assume this custom had been handed down to my parents through generations of fish-eating ancestors. Daddy never questioned why Mom didn't clean the fish that she caught during the day.

After dinner was cleaned up, we would sit around a campfire, sing cowboy songs and tell ghost stories as we listened to the coyotes howl under the stars. It was a pleasant arrangement and worked well for everyone. No one ever questioned the job rotation order, until this fateful trip.

Ex #1 was raised by a wonderful German woman who instilled in him that women had to work as hard as men at the same jobs as men. On the whole I agreed with this. Then, the afternoon of our big catches, Ex #1 questioned our family's status quo of fish cleaning.

Now the problem was he didn't go about it by talking it out in a communal way with Mom, Daddy and me. No, he simply took my hook line and dumped it in front of me with a knife. "You caught 'em, you clean 'em."

Rural Genius: Secrets to Long Term Marriages

My parents wisely got busy with other chores and stayed out of this little drama.

I was completely embarrassed at what I perceived as his incredibly rude behavior. I did the only thing that a good southern woman could do—I turned my back to him.

Big mistake.

He took my arm and swung me back around saying, "Clean your own fish."

Good southern women are taught never, I mean never, to fight in public. There is a code of silence when it comes to arguing in public. I guess Ex #1 didn't get that memo. The only recourse I felt I had was to kneel down and start cleaning the damned fish. There was only one problem, I'd never cleaned a fish before.

Men who go fishing without women are very self-reliant, they catch, clean, cook and clean up all on their own. But I was from a long line of pioneer rancher women who had always had a man to do the fish-cleaning for them. Oh, I suppose my great-grandmother, Mama, probably could clean a fish, then again, there's not a lot of water where they lived in New Mexico.

Hmm, maybe she never even ate a fish!

Alas, here I was, avoiding a fight and the embarrassment of letting my parents know I had a less-than-perfect marriage. Plus, I was trying to intuitively guide my hands to cut off the fish head from memory of watching the men perform this function.

Ex #1 intervenes and says, "You've got to scale the fish before you

Hilda Carpenter

cut off the head, silly."

By this time, Mom and Daddy were clearly uncomfortable and protective of me. Daddy just shook his head and all I could see was the top of his hat as he cleaned fish. Mom came over to try to help me, but, good grief she'd never cleaned a fish either! This poor dead animal was being mauled by two women bent on keeping the peace with Ex #1.

Ex #1 turns to Mom, "Don't help her, she needs to learn how to do this."

No one had ever stood up to my Mom, so she was struck dumb by his rudeness. Again, remember we're Southern women, we are taught to respect elders while we are in the womb.

I guess Ex #1 read a look of venom on Mom's face. I was too afraid of her to look up and witness her mauling Ex #1 to death.

My Mom's expression, or some sort of fear brought out a "kindness" in him—he decided that he'd teach me how to scale the fish.

Did I say kind? Well, he wanted to help me. Husbands should never try to "teach" their wives anything.

Now I had a gazillion scales on my hands and as he brought his face close to the scaling project to correct my technique, I calmly slid my scaled-slimy hand down his face. Not just the cheeks, I mean the from the forehead to the chin.

I thought he was going to kill me right then and there. He might have, had my parents not been within strike range with their knives.

My mom had to turn around and hide her laughter as Ex #1 turned so dark I thought he was going to pop.

It was a good bet that he was going to become Ex #1, or I was going to die, when I made the fatal mistake of giggling. I often giggle at inappropriate times, and this one was a whopper of a bad time.

Needless to say, Ex #1 walked off. I kept on cleaning my fish and did not complain when a few of the bites of cooked fish had some interesting texture.

Ex #1 was smart enough, as were my parents not to complain either, or I would have probably busted a gut laughing. And most likely have been killed in my sleep.

Blending Families

The chances of a failed marriage are 50%. This statistic alone indicates that you may be in a relationship where you, or your partner has been divorced. There is a high probability that you or your partner may have children from the previous marriage.

The next few comical stories are about exactly this scenario. I include them in this book as a tribute that blended families can still mean a long-term relationship. Of course, previous marriages and previous children complicate the scenario and can certainly mean that you have less chance of having a low-conflict relationship. Ex spouses always tend to muck up the works, no matter how well you get along with them.

I know a person who maintained a friendship with her ex-husband's two previous ex-wives long after her divorce. The only thing these ladies have in common is who they chose to marry. They laugh about if they could have just compared notes with each other, before they married him, they could have saved themselves the divorce. The first ex-wife said, "That's not fair, I was the first ex." She has a point.

It's always interesting to compare notes with your partner's ex(es). It's too bad you can't have those conversations before you marry. Well, if you did compare notes, most likely you would still be blinded to the common relationship themes. In other words we naturally want the Ex to be the villain.

If you decide to marry someone who has an Ex, try your best to make friends with that person. Why? Well, most likely if you can remove the blinders, you will discover that she or he already knows a lot of themes that will come up in your own relationship. For example, if your future husband/wife cheated on their ex, then there is a good chance they will cheat on you. Same thing for money trouble or any specific theme that broke their marriage apart. A good rule is to seek the information you don't want to see.

Here's an example, a woman who was terribly in love with a man who had divorced twice. He claimed that both women had their own problems that led to the failures. Now, on one hand this could mean that he is naive about how he chooses a mate. On the other hand it may indicate that he always looks for excuses for failures in other people. In either case, it means that he has a flaw in his personality.

For me, I had two Ex's and Hubby had one ex. I knew that I had to do a lot of work on myself, because a person who has multiple failed serious relationships has a major personality flaw. Hubby was so enamored with me he simply made excuses for me. Ok, let's face it that made my day, it was great to hear someone else talk trash about my ex's. But I had to work really hard to ignore hubby and to keep looking at what were the central themes to my marriage failures. What I discovered in this process were two things.

First, I didn't always tell my Ex's what I thought. I believed that keeping a quiet, calm environment was more important. Then, when I finally had "stuffed" my feelings enough, I exploded. This stuffing was a learned flaw from my own parent's marriage. I needed to learn how to communicate my feelings without fear that I would upset the apple cart. Three marriages later, I realized that sometimes the apple cart needs to be upset in order to identify the rotten apples in a relationship.

Second, the central value around money management was not shared by Ex #1 and Ex #2. In both cases, I ignored the warning signs that my Ex's didn't share my own need to have security about money. If they overspent (especially if it was for me), I saw that as generosity, not irresponsibility. If they told me we could afford it, I believed them. In both cases of my first 2 marriages, the difference in how we valued money was a major destruction to my relationships.

So, I watched Hubby's money management and values long before I agreed to marry him. I also was aware that he tended to stuff his feelings. This meant that I would always need to be guarded to not stuff my own feelings and to ensure I kept checking in with him about his true feelings.

In the case of my blended family with Hubby, there was no way to really know how the relationship would grow or dissolve between hubby and my children, and me with his. I went ahead and married him because I saw in him the desire for a family, including my own children. I felt comfortable that I could be the step-mom to his children and love them like I loved my own children.

I often see blended families pretend they love each other's

children, but in reality, they will always love their children a little more. I knew I could discipline all 4 of our children equally the same. For hubby, he had to work at this one and we worked on it together. What this looked like was having conversations about how he treated his children as guests so they would see him as a good dad. When he treated them as guests, my children became confused why their step-siblings didn't have to do chores, etc. Thankfully, he was able to see this in himself and made his own course correction. If he had not been able to do that course correction, our family-values would have caused us a lot of trouble.

In my clients, this phenomenon shows up when the two parents are not equally disciplining the children. For example, one parent is the "easy" parent while the other one is the "hard" parent who must make the kids behave. The best scenario happens when both parents equally share the parental burden of making difficult choices for their children.

The step-children might resent the new parent, especially when that new parent starts becoming involved in disciplining them. However, if their own parent backs the step-parent, the kids cannot triangulate and manipulate the two parents into choosing sides. As soon as a parent chooses the kids over their spouse, a problem-wedge forms that will only grow as the child learns more creative ways of manipulation.

Hilda Carpenter

Meeting Hubby's Ex after Tequila

Tequila is a very interesting alcoholic drink. It's made from agave cactus leaves. If it is really good, it's great to just sip with a slice of lemon and a tad of salt. The best thing about tequila is you don't have any idea how much you drank. Until you stand up.

I moved to California from Texas into a beautiful house that had several lemon trees in the back yard. On one day, my friend (who later became Hubby) came over. Like any good woman raised in the South, I made some lemonade. It was a beautiful northern California day with mild temperatures, blue skies, sweet flower-air, green trees and grass. Our four kids decided it would be a lot of fun to play croquet, so out came the croquet set. The lemonade cooled down and stimulated the kids (because it's made with a ton of sugar if it is done right). Eventually, Hubby and I sat on the porch to watch them play. It was a good day.

Once the lemonade was gone, I remembered that I had a half of a bottle of tequila sitting idle in the pantry. So, I cut up the lemons, brought out some salt and proceeded to teach hubby how to drink tequila shots. He's a quick learner! Before long, we had solved the worlds problems and were giggling at the cute, darling children.

About an hour or so later, it was time for hubby to take his kids back over to his ex's. So, we stood up. We immediately had to catch each other before we could take a step.

Oh dear—never stand up after you drink tequila.

Somewhere in that mix, Hubby had the common sense to call his ex and her new husband to come pick up the kids (according to my friend, she moved her buddy into Hubby's old house before their divorce paper's ink dried So over the tequila, we decided we

Rural Genius: Secrets to Long Term Marriages

didn't like her very much, or my 2 Ex's either). If you didn't know mixing Tequila and gossiping about Ex's can make anyone mean.

Putting my meanness aside—(well, I wasn't going to be the bitch, and as any good Southern woman knows, you always smile at someone you don't like, Bless Their Hearts). Well, they arrived and I, being the friendly, extroverted Texan, went out to welcome them to my home.

"Hi! I'm so happy to meet you two!"

I made the "no-no" sign as I pointed my finger between the two of them.

"He has told me ALL about YOU!"

At the time when these words came out of my mouth, I didn't think about the implications that my words might have on the situation between Hubby's ex and her new husband.

Silly me, in my tequila stupor, I couldn't figure out why they were so unfriendly.

About 3 am the next morning, I wake up in a panic! Hubby had stayed over for the first time. I saw him in my bed and yelled, "Oh MY GOD!"

Stone sober at this point, I asked him if I should call his ex tomorrow and apologize, because I realized how inappropriate my greeting had been.

He nearly fell out of the bed laughing, snorting, "Absolutely not! I thought it was perfect!"

I was not convinced, I mean good grief, her children were at MY home, the new friend (er— by 3 am, girlfriend), who was clearly inebriated and rude to boot.

I never did apologize, trusting hubby to tell me the truth about what would be appropriate. The kids evidently raved to their mom about the wonderful time they had had at my house and what a good cook I was (Hell, I didn't even remember cooking!).

So, hubby's ex and I have always had a bit of a standoff relationship. And I NEVER, NEVER ever say to someone I just met, "I'VE HEARD ALL ABOUT YOU!"

Good grief.

Oh, and I lay off the tequila shots.

"Jose Cuervo, you are a friend of mine … did I dance on the bar, did I start any fights?" —— Shelly West

Rural Genius: Secrets to Long Term Marriages

M&M's

My daughter was a darling 2-year old when Hubby and I first met and became friends—before he eventually became Hubby. I called him "Hunk" because, well, he was one.

We would often gather up our four kids (we both had two kids). My daughter absolutely loved him from day one.

I had a little Ford truck that could barely fit me and my two kids, so we would typically take his sedan on our adventures. All of our friends from work would meet us where ever we were going. If we went to the beach, Hunk would always spend hours returning his car to pristine condition. I mean there was no grain of sand left by the time he finished. He was meticulous that way, which is pretty impressive with kids.

On one such outing to the beach, the trunk was full of towels, toys and beach paraphernalia. The boys were hungry (weren't they always?), so we stopped to get Burger King. As it turned out they had some little packages that included a burger, chips and a small package of chocolate, M&M's.

After finishing the meal, we loaded back up into the car and headed out. Of course the boys and Hunk's daughter finished up all of their meals in the restaurant, but my daughter had not finished her M&M's. I figured she could eat them at the beach. Hunk said, "Oh go ahead and let her have them now, they'll get all gritty at the beach."

I rolled my eyes as I looked over at him and said, "Are you sure?"

Hilda Carpenter

"Sure! Melts in your mouth not in your hand!" He was in a really good mood ready for the latest adventure.

As soon as my daughter heard this she started reaching for the M&M's. Outnumbered, and after all it was his car, I said, "OK."

We traveled down the road, the kids singing songs, playing games. Suddenly they were all giggling and trying to keep it quiet. Anytime kids get quiet, they need to be checked, so I looked back to check on them.

What I saw was the object of their hysterical laughter—the back seat was smeared with chocolate. My daughter's face was brown, there was chocolate in her curly, blond hair and smeared all over her tiny hands. I turned back forward and tried to figure out a way to tell Hunk so that he wouldn't freak out and wreck the car.

"Uh, Hunk? You may want to pull over so I can get the wipes out of the trunk." So, he slows the car and pulls to the side.

Then he turns around. I thought, oh my God he's going to freak.

He smiles at my daughter and says, "Don't you know M&M's are supposed to melt in your mouth not in your hands?"

She gave him the biggest, chocolately-toothy smile. He turned back around and got back on the road.

I have no idea how long it took him to get all the chocolate stains out of his car and figured we'd never be invited back into the car again.

But, my daughter had him wrapped around her little chocolate finger. I'm happy to say the adventures continued long after that day.

However, Hunk didn't let her eat M&M's in his car ever again.

Mama Bear, Papa Bear, Baby Bear: Who protects whom?

When Hubby and his kids joined my little family, we were all pretty happy. My son, daughter and I were delighted to welcome Hubby's two children into our lives, and what can I say, it was darned nice for my kids to have a responsible man who cared for them.

Everything went pretty swimmingly all around. Until it didn't. I think what I learned during that period, is Hubby was about as left-brained as I was right-brained. He likes to control things, I am more spontaneous. He and I both were incredibly insecure about who and how we were. The bad thing about being insecure is we overcompensated on the things we were not insecure about.

Confused? Yeah, so was I.

My daughter, who was nearly 3 when hubby and I joined up loved for me to carry her around—constantly. She would hold up her arms and I would immediately pick her up. If I needed both hands/arms, like to cook dinner after a long day of work, I would tell her to hold on like a monkey. At that point she would wrap her little legs around my waist really tight, and wrap both her arms around my neck, thus relieving me of the necessity of holding her, and not dropping her on the floor. This worked really well because I could have her close to me and have both hands to work. Now, in those days, they had not invented all the really cool ways to tote your kids around with papooses, or whatever those wrap things are. Much less the very cool kid backpack carriers. My peer parents, like me, built up a lot of arm muscles and core body strength. The only time I was not delighted to tote my daughter around was when my daughter was really whiny. That irritating, right-at-my-ear whine, splitting my ear drum was not fun—at all. Of course, if I tried to put her down, she would throw a grand-champion temper tantrum. I was certain the neighbors were going to come over with the Child Protection Services to investigate how I was killing my daughter by letting her have her tantrum.

If we were in the grocery store, I'd just let her whine in my ear. No way was I going to subject the other shoppers to her well-developed voice, arms and legs. On top of the noise, she would buck, so we really were in danger of me dropping her right on the bin of tomatoes.

Oftentimes, we bought toast and milk for dinner and no produce. The produce aisle seemed to attract tantrum babies, not just mine. Do grocery stores use a special pheromone in that aisle? (Like Vegas does to get you to gamble more?) Well, as any mother knows, this too shall pass—

For Hubby, he was particularly good at problem solving and wanted to control my daughter's neediness. Instead of taking the attitude of "this too shall pass," he wanted to fix the situations that would arise between mother and daughter. This was a big mistake.

The best way I can explain the dynamic that goes wrong in these scenarios is with the children's story, the three bears. You've got Papa Bear—his job is to make sure the family is safe and cared for. He has a particular interest in ensuring Mama Bear's happiness. So when Papa Bear sees Mama Bear frazzled, he zeroes in on Baby Bear. Baby Bear becomes threatened that Mama Bear is going to go away. Baby Bear doesn't want this because, Mama

Hilda Carpenter

Bear tucks him in at night, sings to him, and cooks the porridge. Mama Bear's job is to protect Baby Bear, so when Baby Bear gets distressed at the thought of losing Mama Bear, Mama Bear goes after Papa Bear with a vengeance. Ya just don't mess with Mama Bear…

So, back to overcompensation. Left-brain Hubby wants to find a forever solution to my daughter manipulating me to get my attention. He keeps taking her and putting her down to walk, saying, "You have two legs!" He did this with great aplomb, but my reaction was the opposite of what he wanted.

I became even more protective of her, thus the daughter wins, every time.

Beyond financial stress, the most stress that occurs in a marriage, at least in my experience, is dealing with the children. We finally figured it out, but my blind side was I didn't want to believe I was being manipulated. Hubby didn't want to be seen as weak. Jeez, no wonder it took us years to figure this out.

And all the time Baby Bear is saying, "My porridge is Juust Right!" Because Baby bear typically gets her way.

Rural Genius: Secrets to Long Term Marriages

When One Works We all Work

I grew up in a household that my mother did most of the chores. She would vacuum, or mop as my siblings and I watched TV. She would cook a full dinner for the 5 of us and clean up afterward. She would mow the lawn, drive us to whatever appointments we had (before we were licensed to drive). She rarely took naps, and she always had donned makeup, a dress, and a smile for when Daddy came home from the fields. She sounds perfect, right? Wrong. I was completely unequipped to face my life after marrying Ex #1. He had a tenet he learned from his mother that did not afford the wife to go off to play bridge (like Mom did), or play golf (like Mom did). My Daddy was very accommodating to my mother's lifestyle of play. Oh she worked hard, as I've said, but she played hard too. So what I grew up with was a hard-working homemaker who didn't have a career. Nice work if you can get it.

Shortly after my marriage and disastrous honeymoon with Ex #1, he informed me that I had to get a job. That he was in no way going to support a lifestyle like my mother and grandmothers had. I felt like a cement bag had landed on my head. I didn't even know how to go about looking for a job, much less securing one. But secure one I did, working for Olan Mills, a high-volume photography studio. My job was to go down the phone book (we didn't have personal computers in those days), cold call the person who answered and try to get them to come into the studio to have their picture taken. My supervisor was quite delighted when I suggested that I get the local University's phone book and sell the students on the idea of having their portrait taken to give to their parents for Christmas. It was dang hard work, required the courage of David, and forced good diction on the telephone.

I came home exhausted on the first day of work. When Ex #1 arrived home I so proudly announced that I had gotten a job and worked that day. He was thrilled, then he asked me who I worked for? I proudly told him, "Olan Mills."

The ridicule dripped off his voice with a savory hint of disdain as he said, "A telephone solicitor? You got a job as a telephone solicitor?"

Well, I didn't know what a telephone solicitor was until that moment, nor did I have any idea that they were the bottom feeders of the job market. Truth be told, it's probably one of the hardest jobs I have ever had in my career and it only lasted a day. I immediately quit based on his disapproval. When I called my supervisor the next day, she expressed her disappointment, because I was one of the hardest workers she had ever had.

We can thank my Daddy for that. He always told me that people always want a good hand, who can work hard, with a pleasant attitude. He was right. If I could make it at Olan Mills, then I could make it anywhere, right?

Ex #1 decided he needed to coach me on the types of jobs I should try for: bookkeeper, clerk, maid (but only for a very fine lady), not a car salesman, or insurance salesman, or anything that might be seen as pushy.

Ok, I had been phenomenally good at math in High School, so I

Rural Genius: Secrets to Long Term Marriages

went after bookkeeping jobs. I landed my first bookkeeping job for a loan shark company. I say loan shark in that only people who could not get credit from banks got loans from this company. But, it fit the profile of someone Ex #1 could admire. I mean after all, his mother worked as a bookkeeper during the day, and tended bar at nights. It never occurred to me to go to bartending, or waitress school. Unfortunately, to find this bookkeeping job I went through a job placement service. They garnished my wages for the first 3 months, thus I made approximately $1.00 every two weeks. What a deal. But ex #1 was happy because I was a working woman. I fell deeper, and deeper into depression, but had no idea that there was a way to seek help. Ex #1 was my beginning and end. Three months into the marriage, the government disbanded the Viet Nam War draft. Ex #1 immediately quit college, even though he only lacked 6 units to graduate. He blew off the Air Force recruiter who had signed him up to keep him from having to go into the Army. He determined that we would move to South Texas and he would go to work in a Good Year Store as a clerk. Why would he do clerking? I mean he had a job in the computer department as a computer operator for Ma Bell, for goodness sake. Well, he made this choice based on the fact that his brother was going to open a Goodyear Store and they were going to go into business together.

Only, he never went into business with his brother. We stayed in San Antonio for 3 years. I kept working as a bookkeeper for an oil company, then a waste management company, then finally as the secretary for the Sociology department in a private University. After the three month mark, where I sat on the side of my bed and cried, I decided to live by the adage, "You made your bed, lie in it." So I literally shook off the depression and lived my life with Ex #1.

After three years of working in the Goodyear store, Ex #1 decided he had had enough. He decided that perhaps the farming life that I had left behind was the right life for us. So, we hooked up our trailer, and moved back to West Texas onto my grandparent's land. I went to work for the cotton gin, and he became a farmhand for a dear family friend.

Life was better in West Texas for us. But I grew restless and decided it was time for me to have a baby. My beautiful son was born within a couple of years of our move. Then, the postpartum depression hit me with a thunderclap as loud as those that accompany the dangerous tornadoes when they rip across the fields.

I was trapped. Painfully lonely. Depression is painful, in case you ever wanted to know. The depression was beyond postpartum, because I had a husband that could care less if we had a sex life. He ridiculed me when I dressed up in a neglige and held a bottle of champaigne up while I was standing in front of the TV, trying to get his attention.

Enter, boy-toy. He talked me into leaving my home and running away with him. He was leaving his wife, too. The unfortunate part was that his wife was pregnant. Oh my God, I still cannot believe I was such a cliche. But run away, I did. A year later, I broke up with him and I made amends to the ex-wife of boy-toy, but the damage was done for both of us.

Rural Genius: Secrets to Long Term Marriages

What I got out of that experience, besides a blow to my ego, was a beautiful son, and a great work ethic.

Years, and another ex, later, I met Hubby. He and his kids came over one weekend for a play day for our four children. I started cooking dinner, vacuuming, mopping, etc. Then hubby says to the kids, "When one works, we all work."

All I could do was stare at him. Here was a gorgeous man, who worked along side of me. He put the kids to work setting the table. He taught his kids and mine how to do their own laundry. We instigated a rule that whoever cooks doesn't have to clean up. This meant that we needed to teach the children how to cook a simple meal. Then he and I would clean up after them while they got to watch television, or go outside and play.

As I juxtapose my mothers' life to mine, I think the idea of "when one works, we all work" serves everyone better. It prepares the kids to be independent and responsible. It teaches them not to take someone for granted for any work that they do.

Yeah, "when one works we all work" kept hubby and I together through some pretty rough years.

Canoes and Coordinating Disasters

If you ever want to know how well you and your partner work together, get in a canoe with a third person, like a surly teenager. Even the most even-keeled family will explode.

The canoe exercise works like this: each person takes turns at being at the front, the back and the center positions of the canoe. The middle person's job is to stay perfectly quiet and be the conscientious observer during the battles that will always ensue between the front and back man. It sucks to be in the middle. Trust me, this exercise will bring out the worst in everyone, and you'll get to see how your family acts out under stress.

Hubby and I had this terrific experience at a weekend retreat with Teen. The objective was to cross a very shallow lake that was incredibly cold. For those of you who never have travelled and camped out in northern Maine in September, trust me, the ground and water are very, very cold. To add to the delight of the retreat, there were about 5 other families with us. Each family consisted of Mom, Dad and Teen. We were excited to go because our relationship and communication among the three of us had so greatly improved. Hubby and I were reconciled and together after our separation. Our family was looking very strong. I was quite proud of myself for holding us all together.

Yeah, I know I was a jerk like that. Then this experience made me humble.

Night one, we pitch our little, itty, bitty, bitty (did I mention it was small?) tent. Evidently it was too early to be able to stay in the yurts. September is still considered Summer in northern

Rural Genius: Secrets to Long Term Marriages

Maine. Now, trust me, September/Summer on the northern Maine-Canadian border is an oxymoron for anyone who lives in the south or California. It's darned cold. Oh I guess I mentioned that already, didn't I?

Well, after pitching the tents, we all start looking for firewood. Nature began calling us, and the facilitators explained the potty rules. You had one place to poop and another place to pee. This confused me completely, because to my knowledge I had never had to bifurcate my toilet activities. I could not concentrate on gathering the right kind of wood because, I was completely distracted obsessing on how to poop without peeing and vice versa.

So, by the time I brought my share of the firewood, I had collected all the wrong type of wood and had to start over. Great, we're off to a wonderful start here, I can tell. First of all, I've decided I'll just hold my pee and poop for three days, and second, that I would "help" someone who was picking up firewood, so I'd be sure to get the right kind of wood.

The next item for our schedule was dinner. Of course I decided that I would just fast for the weekend and avoid the toilet dilemma. While a couple of families coordinated the preparation of dinner, without talking to each other (part of the stress exercise) the rest of us got to go dig the toilet. It's called a biffy, in case you've never been in Girl Scouts and had to do this process before. Gross. Bodily functions were definitely off my to do list.

By the time we returned to the campsite from digging little holes in the frozen ground, the fire was going and the food was smelling pretty darn good. So, of course I ate. What we witnessed was the disconnect that this poor family had in agreeing who would fix what, and how. The coordinators had given us menus and the food, but each family was responsible for cooking at least one meal together. That first night, the family who prepared dinner smoothly built the fire, prepared and served a delicious meal. Didn't look that hard. Of course they were all mad at each other, but I viewed it as a success—the food was good.

Then it was "sharing" time. Oh Lord save me. When it came my time to share, I suggested rather than bearing our souls to one another, we should just tell ghost stories, or make up a ghost story about the family that killed itself during one of these retreats.

No one thought my idea was remotely funny.

During sharing-time, out comes the ammo that either the teen, mom and/or dad had held in check—possibly for months. Holy cow, everyone was angry. Then it was time for bed. I was stuck between angry Hubby and angry Teen. Joy. The ground was positively freezing and I could not get warm. And to boot, I needed to pee. I decided it would be better to hold it, because if Hubby and Teen were left alone in the tent, they WOULD become the ghosts of people who killed each other.

After the sleepless, pee-less night, freezing my ass off, it was finally morning. Another family had breakfast duty, so again, we had a delightful meal out in the crisp, sparkling, freezing air. At least we didn't have to do the round-the-campfire debrief. Thank God, I don't think I could have taken that so early in the morning. I've never been a morning person in the first place, and I had a stomachache from holding my bladder all night.

Then, it was time to unload the canoes.

Rural Genius: Secrets to Long Term Marriages

I operated a canoe back when the earth was cooling in the 1950's, so I felt confident that I would be proficient (a very desirable state when you have all those angry families around you). We pulled our assigned canoe into the water and all three of us managed to get in the boat without tipping us over. Whew! We were doing great!

First leg of the journey, I was in the front and Teen was in the back, with Hubby silenced in the middle. The interesting thing about a canoe, is it doesn't move straight forward. Go figure. To achieve forward motion, coordination has to occur between the rudder and the power pull of the front person. If the person doesn't have enough power to pull the boat through the water you go slower, duh. If the person in the rudder position doesn't coordinate his movements with the front person, then any sort of strange canoe activity can happen. The canoe can sit still, even though both rowers are working up a sweat that would rival Arnold Schwarzenegger in his body building days. Or, the canoe will go around in circles, it can even go backward (which to this day cannot I figure out how that happened, admittedly, I'm not a physics whiz).

Second leg, I was in the back, Hubby in the front, Teen in the middle. We made forward progress, at a pretty good clip because Hubby is very, very strong. I watched him like a hawk so that my movements would coordinate with his pull stroke. Wohoo, we might even be able to pull a skier at the rate we were going. We pulled ahead of all the other families and made it to the next stop. Then, it was time for the third leg of the voyage: Teen to be in the rear, Hubby in front, and me in the middle.

The third leg, we were going along at a pretty good pace, because as I mentioned Hubby is very, very strong. Then suddenly Hubby yells at Teen about how the teen is killing him by taking away all the advance every time Teen put the oar into the water. What he said was, "Teen, you are sabotaging me!" He started rowing again. Teen started the rudder stroke—

This is when I discovered that the canoe can actually go backward if the front and rear are not coordinated. At that point, hubby snarled loud enough that the Moose disappeared for fear that they might get eaten by big, bear of a Hubby. Teen immediately put it's oar on its lap, matching Hubby's tantrum.

This is the point that I realized the word "silence" meant more than no noise. Silence can also be very loud, stifling tension.

All the other canoes were about a quarter of a mile away, and reaching the next stopping point. We were dead in the water.

Since I couldn't talk, I just looked longingly at the shore and tried to figure out how deep the water was. I'm thinking that maybe I could slosh over to that shore about quarter of a mile away. The water was crystalline clear. Yeah, I could probably do it. This is when I learned the full truth about dissociation of personality. Part of me was already out of that damned canoe and on the shore laughing at these three idiots in the damned canoe. I had an out-of-body experience that felt great.

I turned my head when I heard the two coordinators call out, "Do we have a problem here?"

Immediately I was off the imagined shore and back in the center, unable to talk. So I silently affirmed we did by I pushing my chin up above the top of my head, then slamming my chin in between my boobs. I repeated this several times to make sure the

Rural Genius: Secrets to Long Term Marriages

coordinators knew, "Yes Houston, we definitely have a problem here." Well, duh, I have no idea why I thought I needed to add my antics to ensure they understood the situation. We were in the middle of the lake, no one was happy, and we sure weren't moving toward any goal.

They had to prompt Hubby and Teen a couple of times to talk, all the while I'm exercising my neck up and down. Finally hubby said, "Teen doesn't know how to row a canoe."

Oh boy.

The coordinator asked Teen, "Is that true, do you feel you don't know how to row a boat?"

Teen says, "I did before now."

I now have added lifting my shoulders to the top of my head to get across to these idiot coordinators that we needed an intervention on their part. I was turning blue from holding my breath to keep from talking. On top of turning blue, all the thoughts about crossing the lake on foot made me need to pee.

Alas, no, the coordinators just sat there—exponentially increasing the loud, I mean very loud, silence.

Then the weirdest thing happened. Hubby put his oar back in the water, and Teen followed suit. They never said a word to each other—for 15 VERY LONG minutes. Well, the good news, I thought, at least I don't have to get wet and I can pee soon.

After the 15 minute hiatus Hubby says, "Teen, I think we are getting better at this. What do you think?" The most amazing thing was he didn't have any sarcasm in his voice.

None at all.

Teen answers, "Yeah, I think you're right, yay us!" Again without a trace of sarcasm or disdain.

I was surprised I didn't look like a balloon that has had it's air released—zipping haphazardly in the air as I let out my breath through puffed up cheeks.

What the heck just happened?

That night it was sharing time again. I couldn't wait to see what Hubby and Teen were going to say. I had my words all locked and loaded this time! But I again was amazed, they talked about how well they had worked through the problem and how it helped that I had not talked.

Huh?

Lesson? We all showed each other the worst of ourselves during a stupid canoe journey.

My lesson? Keep up the neck and shoulder exercises and breathe through my nose when they are in conflict. I'm not supposed to fix other peoples' problems. Go figure.

So, if you really want to find out how healthy your relationship is, then go to northern Maine in September, camp out on the ground, hold your pee figure out how to poop without peeing — and get in a canoe.

Rural Genius: Secrets to Long Term Marriages

Don't invite me.

Hilda Carpenter

Circling the Drain

On both sides of my family we are a tad, shall I say, dramatic? Drama is at the root of a lot of families, but both my mother's and father's side had more than their fair share of drama queens and kings. So, naturally, drama was normal for me. In Hubby's case, his family was very, very stoic. Arguments were never held "out loud" nor loudly, so to speak. They simmered and boiled under the surface.

Reconciling our different upbringing's in how we fought was extremely confusing to both of us when we were first together.

One of the things I was absolutely guilty of was overdramatizing the consequences of things that had not yet happened. One of the things that hubby was guilty of was ignoring issues until they blew up. Duh.

It took us years to meet somewhere in the middle. He became better at expressing his emotions before we hit the boiling point, and I became better at waiting until there was actually a problem to work on.

Confusing? Yeah, it was.

For example, about the time that the kids reached the age to get their driver license, I decided we needed to take them out to learn how to drive a standard (stick-shift) car. Hubby thought that this was silly, because most likely they would take their test with an automatic transmission car. The sillier he thought it was, the more determined I was to teach them.

Rural Genius: Secrets to Long Term Marriages

I yelled things like, "I knew how to drive a tractor — that you have to shift — by the time I was 8 years old."

He would calmly say, "I don't think the kids are going to have to drive any tractors, because we aren't farmers."

His calmness ab-so-lute-ly infuriated me. I guess I felt like he wasn't listening to me. Of course I wasn't really telling him what was in the back of my mind: *They are stranded on a desert island, one of them is hurt, they need to get their sibling to the hospital* (yeah, I have hospitals on my deserted island)*, and the only car available to them is a stick-shift. If they don't know how to drive the stick shift, then their sibling will die from their horrible wounds* (where they got their horrible wounds, who knows how, but who cares, they are *DYING*?).

I would absolutely infuriate him because I would repeat my argument over, and over and over (I'm sure hubby was thinking, isn't she ever going to shut up?—but he was smart enough to keep that thought to himself).

Then, one day he said, "You are circling the drain again."

What the heck did that mean?

I said, "I don't care what you think, I'm taking the kids out to teach them how to drive a stick-shift." I mean did he not know that I still had them maimed and dying with no way to get to the hospital?

"You are fixing a problem that they don't have."

What the HECK did that mean?

"It is a problem when they someday need to drive a car that has a manual transmission!!!" I shrieked.

"Huh?" I swear his mouth actually opened into an "O" but uttered no sound after his question.

After he composed himself, "Why do you know that will happen?" He honestly could be so dumb sometimes, but I decided to answer him:

"I don't know it will happen, but I believe they should know how —just in case."

Why did my answer sound so pitiful when I said it out loud? That was the first time I had a glimpse of what he meant by "circling the drain."

Well, I did teach my children how to drive a standard with my little Honda and later a Miata ... I'm quite sure they never drove a standard transmission in all of their adult life.

So, slowly and patiently, hubby taught me to solve problems that were immediately in front of me ... rather than circling the drain of all the horrible things that could happen one day.

So, slowly and patiently, I taught hubby to ask me questions, because I learned that I typically will start a conversation in the middle and not give him any idea of what is going on inside my head.

Sigh, this took years.

Rural Genius: Secrets to Long Term Marriages

And the process continues.

Hilda Carpenter

Sister

My sister's 25 year marriage ended—badly. She was devastated and living in Portland, ME, not the place to be when you are depressed. Her beautiful, 3 story, ranch home, a classic in the area, became a trap for her. She had tons of friends, as is prone to happen anywhere, because she is likable. Although, even her deep friendships didn't salve her pour, embattled soul.

She called me crying several times. It sometimes was hard to even understand what she was saying through her sobs. My heart ached for her sadness, and her aloneness. In one such conversation that had gone on for about 2 hours, I suggested to her that she come out for a visit. "You are going to live a very large life, but I'm not sure Maine is where you will find it." She cried harder.

Each night she would call, I would encourage her to come out to see us, check California for a potential place she could begin anew. I mean after all, most people who migrate to California are looking for something new, great, big that will introduce them to cultures and food that they have heretofore been missing. In fact, it is hard to find a born and raised Californian. If you do find one, ask for their autograph.

The thought of moving was too much for her to handle. I said, "Just pack a bag for a couple of weeks, have a vacation, Hubby and I will take care of you."

"Just pack a bag?" She whimpered.

"That's it." I replied.

It took about two weeks before she decided she could pack a bag, get on a big old airplane and travel to San Jose, the heart of the Silicon Valley. I assured her that when I moved to California in 1984, it was the beginning of a wonderful career and life. I also assured her that she didn't have to stay, or move here. I wanted to care for her in her poor, miserable state. "Families do that for each other." I said, "Families are the most important thing in life. We're your family."

"What about Hubby? Will he mind me being there?"

Since I'd already cleared it with Hubby (the visit anyway), I told her, "He loves you. He can't wait for you to get here. Just let us know when your plane is arriving."

She packed that big old bag. We drove out to Norm Minetta Airport (at that time it only had one terminal) and awaited her flight. Of course, in those days, we could actually go to the gate to be her welcoming party, complete with our dog. She was bringing her dog. A sign that she might be able to hold out for 2 weeks with us.

She never went back to Maine, even to sell her house and pack up her belongings. She lived with us for over a year, in the room that used to be my daughter's room.

I had pictures of all the family across one of the bedroom walls. She asked me to take them down. She said, "It feels creepy to have all those eyes staring at me while I sleep." Hmm. I'd never considered that aspect. I took them all down. She taped up a map of San Jose on the wall, so she could begin to orient herself to the town.

Some of the things that put strains on marriages are done with the best intentions. The first thing I noticed was she was a "morning person." You know the type, the people who have the magical ability that their eyes open and their brain is fully awake. I've never been, never want to be, never will be that person. Hubby was thrilled because he'd lived with a grumpy morning person for 15 years. He had someone who actually liked to eat breakfast upon arising. Me, I have a cup that says, "Sure, I'm a morning person, after about 11:30 am."

I would struggle awakening to the sound of their laughter and smells of bacon. Sister had given up being a vegetarian several years previous to her current culinary tastes. Thank God for that, because the best thing I can make is called "train wreck" and yes, I can burn boiled eggs—Did you know they actually explode? But that's another story.

One of the things that started to bug me was Hubby kept siding with her. Next, the two of them started making me the butt of their jokes. I'm a pretty good sport, but after a month or so, it was not funny to me.

We were well into 6 months when I pulled Hubby aside. "I don't care if you think I am 100% in the wrong, do—not—side against me."

Rural Genius: Secrets to Long Term Marriages

He was confused to say the least. So, I had to give him the explanation from my side of the street. He was still confused. "Don't you want me to like your sister?"

"Well of course I want you to like her. I love it that you like and love her, she's my sister, she is family. You know what that means to me. But you are MY husband not hers. You need to side with me and stop making me the butt of your jokes."

"We don't do that."

So I had to give him an example. "Remember when you were talking about how I garden?"

"Yes, I think so." He may not have remembered the conversation —I continued with my courtroom-worthy drama.

"OK, you both said that I was watering the garden too much, and that California would eventually run out of water because of my gardening technique."

"Oh yeah, well you do turn it on more than I think you should."

"OK, that's between us, I think I have a beautiful flower garden. She's lived in fricking Maine for the last 25 years, where plants only grow about 3 months of the year. What the Hell does she know about California flower gardens?"

"Oh, I think I'm beginning to see your point." I don't know if he actually understood, or just wanted the conversation to be over. We had this same conversation several times over several weeks.

Men can be so dense sometimes.

Sure enough, we were sitting among my beautiful flowers a couple of months later watching our dogs chase each other around the perimeter of our yard. Sister says, "I think you are not successful at growing verbena because they are receiving too much water."

I looked over at Hubby. He suddenly found great interest in the middle button on his shirt. Pointedly, I said, "What do you think Hubby?"

He visibly gulped, I mean like Adam's apple olympics, "Well, I don't know of any neighbors that can grow it either, no matter what their watering choices."

That would have to do.

Sister started laughing, "Oh come on, Hubby. You know I'm right."

"Er, well, we are sitting among some incredible flowers here. I'm going to have to go with the watering is probably about right."

She was dumbfounded. I was jumping for joy in the inside. I mean I know better than to taunt her when I'm winning. After all, I'm the older sister—something for which I believe she's never

Rural Genius: Secrets to Long Term Marriages

forgiven me. I remained quiet, just waiting to see what would happen next.

Well, what can I tell you, but she just said, "Huh, that's interesting." And dropped the subject.

It took a few more times before she realized that Hubby was going to side with me, he wasn't going to make fun of me at my expense.

After she found her new place and new job a year later, she moved out. Oh we still had dinners and fun times playing games. But we had our solitude back—Hubby and I could make love anywhere in the house again.

I learned a lot through that adventure. First, and foremost, I was right, family is the most important thing in my life. Second, family will move in with you during a crisis. Third, it's important for couples to be very frank with each other, even if it makes waves.

I still adore my sister and to this day, if she needed me, I would open my home again. Hubby, on the other hand, knows that I rule my own house.

Hilda Carpenter

The Big, Big Family Reunion

Growing up I had 12 cousins all about the same age as me. And that's just on my Daddy's side of the family. Every Thanksgiving each of Daddy's four sisters, their husbands and their litter of kids would traverse the desert to GrandPappy and Grandmother's house. They lived in the country with a peach orchard just in front of their house. The rest of the land was surrounded by mesquite trees and rattlesnakes. It was pure heaven.

My grandparents built a house that was large enough to fit all of their children and grandchildren. There were secret passage ways, and each room had windows on three different walls, creating a panoramic view to the outside. This view was spectacular, because in the blue-dusk of evenings, we could climb over each other and watch from a safe spot behind the window as coyotes, bobcats, skunks, armadillos and gargantuan spiders would arrive from the four points of the compass to share the bucket of water that Grandmother always left outside for the animals. It's pretty amazing that no animal eats the other animal when they are dying of thirst.

During the day, we built forts and had dirt-clod wars. That is when I learned that I threw like a girl, according to my brother. However most of my cousins were boys, who had no sisters, so they took special care of me and my little sister to ensure sure we were not left out of the fun. They liked having me on their team, because I had the most devious mind and could come up with plans to get behind the enemy walls and pellet them with dirt clods. Yay, for my team. We decided the losers by which team was dirtiest. By late Thursday morning, we were all required to clean up, wash our hands and faces (this typically ended in a water fight). This suited our parents, because we were providing their entertainment.

Rural Genius: Secrets to Long Term Marriages

Of course by the end of the day's wars, we were starving. My little sister would say, "I stahvin' Grandmother, I stahvin', cain't (yes we pronounced can't as cain't) I please just have some serals?" (In human language she was asking for cereal). Grandmother might have given in, but mother was too worried about my sister ruining her appetite. Mother needn't have worried, my sister was always hungry and somehow managed to stay skinny as an orphan. I hated her for that.

Oh it was delightful fun, no doubt. When Thursday arrived, we all sat down to Thanksgiving dinner. All Grandmother's daughters and my mom worked for a week to present a meal that would be finished in an hour. The ladies cleaned up afterward while the men-folk smoked and solved all the world's problems.

When dinner was set, we all had to sit patiently with our hands in our laps or folded in prayer as Pappy droned on about the Good Lord's blessings. Pappy was a politician, so he could drone with the best of any Democrat.

The hardest part of sitting still was not that any of us disagreed with our thankfulness for the bounty. The hardest part was waiting to eat while torturous smells were fat in our noses from the dishes that teased our appetites. The kids of course sat at folding tables that were squished into Grandmother's large kitchen.

After the drone-prayer Pappy would pronounce, "Let's eat!!" Everything became really quiet except for the clinking of spoons on china digging out the fabulous food and putting it on our china plates. Grandmother always insisted that family reunions required only the best of her dishes and flatware. I suspect even when she was destitute with Pappy during the Great Depression, she still put out her best china that she inherited from her Mother, Mammy Nan.

Hilda Carpenter

Grandmother had a very large dining room where all the adults would sit and (oh my) drink a glass of red wine in celebration of family. The red wine was a big deal, because the early Methodists firmly believed in abstinence. And we had a few Baptists in the family, too. So, it got pretty silly quickly and funnier than hell to watch these tea-totaler folks get high.

During their mini-debauchery, this meant we kids were unsupervised, so except when Grandmother (who was a stickler for manners at all times) came in to refill the bowls in the dining room, our manners were, shall we say nonexistent?

Every year at Thanksgiving until my Pappy died and Grandmother developed dementia, this Thanksgiving meal and play ritual was repeated. This gave me some of the best memories of my life. My cousins and I are still fiercely close and each one carries a piece of memory that we fit back together each time we have a reunion (about every 2 years).

Armed with these beautiful thoughts, when hubby and I moved to Texas from California, we bought land in the country and built a big house that would house all of our four children and their kids. I didn't think too much about being crowded, heck that's what happens at family reunions. We had the beautiful outdoors, cots, beds, bedrolls, tents everything that a reunion could require for a medium sized family. In my mind, the reunion gave our children's children the chance to use their imagination to play out doors, board games, or what ever suited their fancy. In my mind, cousins were the best thing God ever invented.

One of the reasons we moved to Texas was because our kids were located on both coasts of the US. From Virginia to California they lived so far away. So, hubby and I figured we'd build in the middle of the country, so no family would have the hardship of traveling all the way across the country with little kids. From either coast, we were about 3 hours away by air.

Rural Genius: Secrets to Long Term Marriages

I couldn't wait until Thanksgiving to have all my kids together. In fact, it had been years since some of our kids had seen each other, after graduating from High School and College. So, after moving into our new home in August, we invited all the kids to come to our home for a family reunion! They all graciously accepted, and Hubby and I spent hours on the road to pick them up at two different airports at four different times. Each couple had a room to call their own. I figured that the kids would sleep out on the porch or in the great room (where the TV was).

I giggled as I prepared food and beds for their arrival. Oh what fun this was going to be!! I was recreating my childhood's best memory for my grandchildren.

The problem with getting together after years of separation is no one really knows the other person very well. Add the fact that we had a new family member and her son joining us—so they had no early childhood memories in common with us. No problem, I thought, I'll pull out the photos and they will all get tickled telling stories about when they were little.

The first night was an adventure. After long delays and plane changes they were all pretty beat. So, after supper, we visited for a short while and everyone started for their rooms.

This is when the first hitch came in. The two grandsons (who were nearly the same age, but as different as blue and orange) decided, no, it was too dark to sleep outside and there might be bugs. It was "creepy."

Creepy?

Well, OK.

So, I said, "No problem you can sleep in the great room and tell stories about your lives to each other."

Not the thing to say to an 11 and 10 year-old.

Another fact then slapped me in the face. Both the boys are extraordinarily attached to their mothers—so they'd just sleep in the same room as mom. Their moms looked at me like I had a third foot in my mouth for even making the suggestion to separate.

Hmmm.

Well, OK. This meant that an adult couple would be sharing a bed with a pre-teen boy in a room that could comfortably fit 2 people, but not 3.

Oh dear—first sign of reunion trouble.

Quick to adapt, we moved the bedrolls into the two rooms, they'd sleep on the floor. There wasn't enough room for a cot, they could just sleep on the floor. This didn't really bother me, since many of my boy-cousins slept in bedrolls outside with the scorpions, much less on the floor.

At least I was smart enough not to say that bugs crawl on the floor. Good god, we'd probably have had to hang hammocks above the parents' beds.

Then, the next hitch came up. Our daughter and her son decided they would sleep with another family (her brother and his wife and two kids). Oh dear ... this meant that there would be six people sleeping in a room that was large enough to house a couple with a fold out couch for their two little girls.

I drew the line on that one and told them they could sleep in the same room as my other daughter. This meant that three people were going to be sleeping on an air mattress (whereas I figured the two single daughters could share the air mattress). Now, this room is my office, so three people were housed in with all my junk.

I couldn't figure out why the kids didn't want to sleep away from their parents. Then the next-to-youngest granddaughter said, well if the boys don't want to sleep in the great room or the outside, I will!!

For heavens sake, the boys didn't want to have an adventure, they preferred sleeping with their moms, and the younger granddaughter was totally OK with the adventure. Hmmm.

All of this would have been fine if we wanted to have an orgy— but for siblings it was getting pretty ridiculous. Oh well.

Breakfast the next morning, everyone was hungry and in amazingly good spirits. The boys decided since it was light outside, they would go down with their little girl cousin to the creek to catch tadpoles.

My jaw dropped to my ankles as each of the 2 boy's mothers called out as they headed down the hill, "Don't get your shoes dirty!"

Huh? I guessed that clod fights were out at that point.

I climbed down the hill with them and said, "You know boys, you are most likely going to get your shoes dirty when one of you "accidentally" falls into the water, which could happen because it's pretty hot out here. If that does happen, don't worry about it, I'll take care of your moms."

They grinned from ear to ear. Message received! When I left them to return up the hill to the house, I was accompanied by lots of splashing noise echoing up the hill with me!

Score one for Grandmother!

One of my daughters-in-law drinks Starbucks coffee every morning. Hubby's brewed coffee was simply insufficient to satisfy her needs. Besides, I didn't have mocha-grande-no foam-whatever-she-drank.

"No worries," I said, "we have a Starbucks. It's only about 15 miles from here!"

I guess that seemed like an insurmountable distance, because she didn't leave, she sort of snarled.

The end of that day we had a delightful surprise when we realized that our septic tank overflowed. One of the grandsons said while holding his nose, "Ooo smells like dad!"

Great.

After an emergency call to the septic guy — thankfully he resolved that issue.

Then, the restlessness hit. Unlike my childhood, our children have any number of devices to entertain them. I'm not sure we ever said to them, "Go outside and find something to play." I mean, I played with rocks and dirt clods—such was my limited sphere of experience.

So, of course the television came on … loud. One of my sons likes Nascar. Thus, the sounds of droning cars going around in an endless left-turns supplanted the laughter and connections that I had hoped would happen between the kids.

It was time to pull out the secret weapon — I asked them to turn

Rural Genius: Secrets to Long Term Marriages

off the television, that I had something they might get a kick out of. If looks could kill, I swear I thought I had a bunch of spoiled teenagers again, rather than fully grown adults. I needed a NASCAR sponsor to navigate out of this one.

Dauntless, I pushed on and pulled out all of the photo albums.

Immediately they all became animated with stories giving background to each snapshot. I heard about antics that I never knew had happened and laughed hysterically at their laughter. Ahhh, now this is what I remember as the sound of reunions. Laughter and stories.

Having made it through the first photo album they scrambled to the closet where I kept all of the photo albums. As I fixed dinner, I suddenly became aware that the laughter had subsided.

Were they already through the 7 albums, and 5 shoeboxes of loose photos? Were they already out of stories?

Oh no — Shit, they came across an album containing photos of my son's first wedding. It was at the very back of the closet, forgotten. His current wife was not a happy camper. Drat, I know she'll never believe that I intended to pull that one out of that closet before they all arrived. If I'm honest, I had forgotten the darn thing was even in there, but I wasn't about to tell her that.

15 minutes later, my son comes into the kitchen to chastise me about not throwing the album away from his first marriage. "Did you do that on purpose to make my wife feel uncomfortable?"

There was no way I could make this right, so I simply said, "Of course not." Further defending myself (I had learned) would only exacerbate the problem. I just kept on cooking. I couldn't explain that each of the albums were a witness to all the events that had happened to me and my children. That particular album, while not currently germane, was a witness to an important event in my son's life. Even if wife #1 became Ex #1.

Day 3, the reunion was getting pretty old. Hubby and I were already looking forward to them leaving. My grandmother used to quote Ben Franklin saying, "Company is like fish, they begin to smell after three days." She and Ben were right.

I think the only people who had a really good time were the grandkids. Their shoes were ruined, the moms were mad at me for letting them get their shoes dirty, but they had 7 tadpoles that they told me to be sure to keep until they turned into frogs or toads. Thus, I deemed the reunion a success!

One by one we took them to the two airports. With each delivery, hubby and I felt lighter. The house was a total wreck, the new carpet in the bedroom was ruined beyond repair (we found that stain a week later. They tried to cover it with a throw rug.). Still, we successfully completed a family reunion.

This reunion was different than my childhood memories, but it was a reunion. Hubby decided to collect all the digital photos we took during their stay and publish a paperback with all the moments. With each picture he annotated what was special to us about that captured moment.

It was a wonderful tribute to our family. Each of the four families received a copy of the book.

It's been 8 years since that reunion. Three of our 4 kids' have brought their families to visit at least one time since then, with the exception of my son and his wife. My son has come once, but without the wife and family (his wife is the one who saw the previous marriage pictures).

Still, I highly recommend family reunions. My cousins, remaining

Rural Genius: Secrets to Long Term Marriages

aunts and uncles still get together on a bi-annual basis. My children have never joined these festivities, even though my cousin's kids are always there.

I miss my family, but take heart that each one of them has their own unique identity. If they decide it's important to get together with their siblings, they will.

Maybe, just maybe one day they will invite hubby and me. Until then, the next time I offer to host a family reunion with them—

I'm getting them all hotel rooms right next to a Starbucks.

Hilda Carpenter

Pepper's Dog Dooky

My parents never liked pets.

One day my aunt surprised my brother with the gift of a puppy. The surprise was not well-received by my parents. They were aghast at her intrusiveness. Immediately my mother and daddy started declining the gift. My aunt, never to be over-ruled by my parents, put her hands on her hips saying, "Every little boy needs a dog!" By this time, we were already playing with the precious bundle of cuteness. The parents had no choice but to accept.

This was the only pet my brother, sister and I ever had. He was a little terrier mutt and to us a miracle. The dog was a full-fledged family member. Even Daddy couldn't say no to us.

The biggest issue my parents had with our little mutt was he pooped all over the place. One day Daddy came through the front door and stepped right in the poop. Oh that was a dark day. My brother had to clean up the hard wood floor with clorox—that floor never was the same. We kids were all terrified that we, or our little dog (notice how my sister and I now also claimed ownership) was sure to be killed.

Daddy didn't kill us, nor the dog. However, we three became very observant about his bathroom needs. Eventually he was completely potty trained and a delight to have around! He eventually died from old age, and of course my parents never allowed another dog around.

During a recent reunion with our kids, we started talking about the first dog I got when the kids were little, Pepper

Rural Genius: Secrets to Long Term Marriages

As an adult, I always had dogs, then one year I decided my son needed a puppy. We named her a very urbane name, Pepper. She was a salt and pepper miniature schnauzer. Smart dogs those schnauzers. House training was a breeze.

The only problem we ever had occurred when Hubby's son and daughter interacted with Pepper. You see, they had cats in their home. The cool thing about cats is you can set them anywhere, high or low, they'll still land on their feet. One day, our littlest daughter tripped and fell into the deep end of the pool. Our eldest son was quick to respond. He set Pepper down on the rail of the patio fence. She immediately fell off and landed on her head! Hubby started yelling, the daughter was yelling and Son #1 was completely confused as to why the dog didn't stay on the railing.

Now, Pepper recovered from the fall and was truly a delight. She loved playing with the kids and roughhousing or just lying on the couch watching TV with them.

The thing about mini-schnauzers is they have hair not fur. This is great for anyone like hubby who is allergic to dogs and cats. The bad news is their hair grows and needs to be trimmed by a groomer about every six weeks.

Dog grooming, well, it was traumatic for the little dog and the kids were always worried that Pepper was going to be sad at the shop. To ensure she was OK, our kids always insisted on accompanying me to pick her up after grooming. This was a singular delight for them. The reunion was terribly fun for me to watch. Such happiness balled up into a tiny dog when she was rescued from the groomer—even if she did have to suffer the humiliation of wearing the groomer's neck scarf. Oh my, I tell you that dog was just too precious for words. The kids snuggled with her as we drove back home. She would just jump all over them in her glee that freedom brought.

One day after picking up Pepper, the routine of total mutual infatuation was going on in the back seat as we drove home. Then suddenly my daughter started screaming, I mean screaming at the top of her lungs! I looked in the rear view mirror and saw that she was crawling out of the child seat and trying to get up by the rear window. Her mouth was a huge "O" with a piercing scream.

My son started yelling, "No Pepper, NO!!!" I glanced at where he was supposed to be behind my seat, but I saw that he also had escaped his seat belt and his butt was plastered to his side window. My other daughter and son had climbed into the front passenger seat.

I couldn't tell what was happening and we were almost back to the house, so I did what any responsible mother does—I sped up to get home and discover what was going on.

I screeched into the driveway and whipped around to look in the backseat. My son's butt was still plastered up to the back window, his head leaning into the top of the car. My daughter was trying to get out of her window, but the rear windows were locked! Her feet were kicking the back of the shot-gun seat in a manic rhythm.

"DOOTY, DOOTY" she kept yelling—no screaming. "DOOTY DOOTY!!!"

My son kept screaming, "NO Pepper NO!"

Rural Genius: Secrets to Long Term Marriages

The two kids in front couldn't stop laughing.

The dog had a little bit of poop still stuck to her bottom, beyond the huge mound that had been dumped on the bench seat of the car, somehow missing the two older kids' laps.

I started laughing so hard tears were coming out of my eyes. My kids were screaming, "LET US OUT, LET US OUT!!"

I had a car that had child locks. If you have children, you know why you engage those locks. I rarely disengaged them, so it took me a minute to find the lock release. All the while laughing at the dog who was so distressed at having an accident she kept trying to crawl over the kids to get away from the dorky. Her dingleberry was dangerously close to popping off with all the commotion.

The kids started piling out of the car while hysterically screaming at the poor dog. The dog flew (I mean like Underdog, the cartoon character) out of the car and made it to the grass to finish up her business.

Over dinner that night, I recounted the story to hubby. He laughed as hard as I did. The kids couldn't stop their laughter.

Then Hubby paused and stated the obvious, "You might want to let her have a potty break before you put her in the car from now on."

I hate it when he states the obvious.

As the kids reminisced on the story at a recent reunion, I remembered what Hubby said and how much it irritated me. I finally had the chance to get him back, "And you, YOU, all you could do that night was state the obvious, 'let her have a break before driving home!'"

"Well, I was right wasn't I?"

I hate it when he states the obvious. The kids just laughed.

Rural Genius: Secrets to Long Term Marriages

Agapanthus A.K.A. My sons are perfect!

After Hubby and I married, we had four children between us. Two kids each. He had a girl and a boy and I had a boy and a girl. Their ages were 12, 10, 9 and 4 when we joined as a family.

We moved to a lovely townhouse with beautiful greenbelt areas. On the edge of the greenbelt the association had planted about a gazillion Agapanthus bushes, also known as "Lily of the Nile." They bloomed once a year on an incredibly long, sturdy stem out of the iris-like leaves. They didn't really have an aroma, but the balls of flowers looked like 8" purple sparklers. The individual petals radiated from the stem in explosions of little trumpet flowers. Each flower made a bouquet that was about 6-8 inches in diameter. To say it was stunning each Spring, simply doesn't cover the magical effect.

Our boys loved playing outside, and with pre-teen boys, it was good for them to get out and run off their energy. Otherwise we probably would have killed them.

One lovely day I received a telephone call from one of our neighbors. Now mind you, we didn't know any of our neighbors because with 4 kids, busy careers, getting to know neighbors didn't rate high on our list.

When the call came in, I was delighted, because I'm from a little tiny West Texas town, and frankly Californians are not that neighborly. After the pleasantries finished (5 seconds later), she started complaining about my boys. Now if you have ever had boys, you know you're going to get some complaints. These issues come in the form of broken windows, loud noise on the sidewalk from their skateboards, or the always-present "we're learning how to cuss" when the parents aren't around. Any of these events pretty much spell doom for the boys, because the two-hour lecture about being courteous is not far behind.

However, this neighbor said that our precious boy-angels had cut down all of the Agapanthus blossoms.

Well, I was incensed. Of course no child of mine would have done so much destruction. Being the fiercely loyal person and mom, I told her she had made a mistake. I had taught my children to cherish nature, not destroy it. My voice dripped with disdain as I finished my declaration.

She told me, in no uncertain terms, that now the entire neighborhood would be without the beautiful blossoms because they only grew once a year.

I told her in unmitigated terms that we would be among the grieving neighbors right along with her—my boys included. I told her the association had a responsibility to find out who would cause such destruction, but they probably wouldn't because their HOA committee never agreed on anything ("Bless Their Hearts").

Now, boys can be pretty darn sneaky. So I mentioned the neighbor's call at the dinner table that night. I asked the boys if they knew anything about someone cutting down the blossoms. I

Rural Genius: Secrets to Long Term Marriages

stared each one of them down. With a two-pair of wide, rounded, green eyes and blue eyes they solemnly said "No! Who would do such a thing?"

Hubby looked like he was suspicious, but I assured him that I didn't believe the boys would tell such a blatant lie with such innocent conviction. Plus, I had given them the "mom-stare."

Our little brood grew up into fine upstanding citizens, and we get all the kids together as their busy lives will accommodate.

On such a little reunion, my heart warmed as I watched the kids reminiscing with old photo albums from their childhood. In the album were pictures from Easter Sunday when we lived in the townhouse. The boys started giggling like little girls — It's a strange sound coming from men who are bigger than I am. I smiled and said, "what are you two remembering?"

They said in unison, "Karate Kid."

OK, that was slightly confusing. I did remember a movie of that name, but couldn't figure out how it fit in with the memories contained in the album.

I was lying in bed that night around 3 am when it hit me! Karate chops to the Agapanthus.

God parents are so gullible, and should never, never assume their kid is innocent.

Cinamax

Kids just love to hear adults say, "In my day —" Well you're right, they don't. I think I was the only weird kid who loved hearing about the antics of my parents and grandparents who lived in rural settings through the Great Depression. It fascinated me how on earth they could creatively keep themselves occupied.

Then television came along. I remember our first TV, it had a tube that flickered green images. Sometimes we had to adjust the antennae to get one of the three channels available to us. After 10 PM, forget it, there was a screen with a big silent Indian in the middle after the National Anthem to bid us good night. Programming would begin again the next day around 7 am with the news, then soap operas. We didn't really have talk shows back in my day.

My grandparents were one of the first people to get a new, Color TV. Not only did it have gray/silver images, it had COLOR! Man they must have been rich.

My children grew up in the days of cable. The programs never stopped all night long. It was really great whenever they wanted to watch cartoons, they tuned to the cartoon channel (In my day, the cartoons were only on from 7 am to 10 am Saturday).

When they grew into the pre-teens and teen years, they would invite kids over for sleep overs. By that time, we lived in a tri-level home with a gargantuan, rear-screen TV down in the family room. The door shut on this room, so Hubby and I could enjoy a

Rural Genius: Secrets to Long Term Marriages

pleasant evening that was relatively giggle-free. When bed time came, we were a full one-story away from the frivolity.

Before retiring, I always went into in the family room to kiss my son or daughter and bid their guests good night. I might ask them what they planned or when they expected to get to sleep. They typically would say, "We're going to watch a movie then go to sleep."

One of the really cool inventions on cable was premium channels. For a subscription cost you could add these premium channels onto your cable bill. I particularly liked HBO because a movie didn't have commercials. (In my day, the TV movies were black and white and always had commercials.) The new premium channels were typically high-quality and indicative of what you could see in the movie house. Yes, I still call it a movie house.

However, when the cable company called to ask if we wanted to add some premium channels onto our cable, they told me that the premium channels came in packages. So, if you wanted HBO, then you might get Showtime and Cinemax along with HBO for the same package price. My belief is that if you can get a good value, then go for it! Three for the price of one seemed like a pretty good deal to me.

At our last family reunion, I was doing an "In my day ..." droning on about my evolution from black and white TV to cable and now into streaming videos.

My son says, "Oh yeah, I remember those days. Skinomax."

Hilda Carpenter

"What the Hell is skinomax?"

He cuts a glance over to my other son and said, "Should we tell her?"

I indignantly put my hands on my hips and said, "Yes, you should tell me!" The nerve of these kids thinking I'm some old relic that needs editing on what ever stories my kids tell me.

"Skinomax is another name for Cinamax."

"I don't understand." I sensed a huge boulder of dumbness about to fall on me.

"Cinemax only showed R or X rated movies after about 11 pm. So when we told you were going to watch a movie, it mostly likely was a skin flick."

"Oh —My— God!

"You boys were too young for porn. Hell I was too young for porn!" I said this in total shame that I was such a terrible parent, and all the while thinking that I was a loving, trusting, parent to my young kids. Well I was loving, but I had no business trusting a couple of pre-teen boys.

Lesson learned—Never trust anything that comes out of a kid's mouth. Hmm, I think I had to have remedial training on that one lesson.

Rural Genius: Secrets to Long Term Marriages

Multiple times.

Hilda Carpenter

Part 3 Successful Marriages Need Girl Friends and Guy Friends

Hilda Carpenter

Friends who are Girls

I grew up in itty bitty towns, well we didn't know they were itty bitty, I mean we were 3-A schools, for goodness sake. For those of you from big towns that means a rural town in the middle of nowhere, where the football team has to travel about 200 miles for Friday night lights with another little rural town.

But we thought we were big-time.

The thing about social circles in little itty bitty towns is they are small. I guess probably all social circles are small, but when your class size is about 150 people, that means that the cliques are really small, and rattlesnake-mean. There are the typical segregations: jocks, beauty queens, band geeks, and nerds (although we didn't have that word when I grew up, there were just some really smart people who were good at algebra and science).

I was a blend of band geeks and nerds, but somehow the beauty queens thought I was funny, so I got to play on the periphery of their world. In other words, I was a jack of all trades and I didn't really fit in anywhere. High School is no place for a philosopher too young to know how to philosophize.

So, what did I do? I scrambled to fit in. I was the class clown—everyone basically liked me or they didn't. I can honestly say that most people remember me from high school. My claim to fame was that I was brilliant at algebra, a good flutist, and a majorette. In short, a nerd.

My boyfriends were always in the band or in the science club. I played in the pit band while other people took the stage.

Girls were a total enigma to me.

Oh I had one or two friends that I liked, but I always felt awkward and clumsy around any girl. Now, boys, that was a different story. I had an older brother, so I totally "got" boys—that is until they dropped me as a girlfriend to go out with the girl with big boobs, pouty mouth, and who was rumored to "put out." Then I was at a loss. My mother pounded the idea into me that only "bad girls" went beyond kissing on a date. My brother told me that I needed to let boys touch my boobies, otherwise I would be seen as frigid. I was, to say the least, confused.

Was I to believe my mother or my brother? I chose my brother, he may have been a schmuck dating a local punch, but I trusted him more than I did my mother.

My competitive mother and these High School years set the stage for how I viewed women. They were all vindictive liars who would say one thing and mean another. Boys, and later men, were always pretty transparent to me, and I never felt like I got bait and switched because I always knew they just wanted sex. Now women, who knew what the hell they wanted!!

It wasn't until I was in my 60's that I found my tribe, as my friend Chick would call it. I finally figured out that if my friends who were girls were secure, accomplished and smart, they didn't play games. They said what they thought and didn't really care about what other people thought.

My friend Chick is one of the smartest people I know. She doesn't mind telling me things like, "You need to —— or For GODS sake, get some business cards!" I just love that about her. My husband may be a little jealous that I have found a friend that I trust as much as I do him, but he'll get over it, as long as I give him good kisses and let him touch my boobs.

Yes, it is good to have girlfriends. My other friends who are girls kept telling me that, they said, "You should be better about sending birthday cards." Or they would tell me how insensitive I was that I hadn't called to go to lunch.

Chick, she's smart and she has her own life independent of my actions.

Who knew? Not me. Chick is educating me on how it is to be in a friendship with another woman without sexual innuendo, just brains, no venom.

The first time I ever saw her she looked like a movie star surrounded by a flock of hens. She was elegant, poised, and by God, smart. I was totally intimidated.

Just yesterday, I had lunch with her. I told her that I had absolutely no clue how to pick out a formal dress for my daughter's upcoming wedding. I needed her help. I told her I had absolutely no idea how to build a "platform" for my own successful writing. I needed her help.

The most amazing thing about Chick, is she didn't make me feel inferior that I didn't know how to do something at which she was adept. No, rather than taking advantage to further her position, she said, "I can help you with that."

Holy shit. A woman who is willing to help another woman — in

Rural Genius: Secrets to Long Term Marriages

no time in my professional career as an executive had I felt like there wasn't a "quid pro quo" waiting in the wings.

My experience with women executives was that if she and I were in line for the same job, then she would do everything she could to make sure I didn't advance before she did—and leave claw marks on my back.

Feels good to have a friend. I wonder if I were raised in a more mainstream environment rather than a rural environment if I might have discovered this phenomenon before I was 62. I wonder if I had a different relationship with my mother, if I might have learned earlier.

Oh well, I guess that doesn't matter. What I do know is mostly you can't trust women, unless they are so successful as you are that they are not intimidated by you!

Thank you, Chick for opening my eyes and heart!

Guy Friends

My brother had a 56 Ford sedan.

No not the cool one, the one Ford manufactured two or three years after the cool one. His Ford was always needing some kind of repair. For example, if you put it in reverse, there was a very good chance that you could not get the gear to shift back into first, second or third for that matter. If the police saw him driving home from school in reverse, they just figured he was having trouble with the transmission again.

Then there was the other problem: if he got it into 1st, 2nd and then shifted into 3rd, there was a very good chance that the engine hood was going to pop up, thereby blocking his view. When this happened, he had to quickly crank his window down and hang his head out the window to see where he was going. Not fun in the middle of a sand storm in West Texas.

The darn Ford dripped oil like it was a sieve. I can remember my brother buying 10/40W oil by the case, only then needing to replenish his supply of oil the next weekend. Yeah, it was what anyone in their right mind would call a "junker." But it was his and it was blue and it had big, wide seats that he could lay his slutty girlfriend on. Ick.

One weekend, he decided that he needed to pull his transmission and make some repairs. His thought was that he could work on the gears to make sure he could get the car out of reverse when he manipulated the gear shift. Good idea. The previous semester, I had appendicitis. Our mother, the High School Physical Education teacher (another story entirely about how humiliating it is to be a fat girl with a mom who was a PE teacher in my High School), needed to borrow my brother's car to relieve my Daddy from hospital duty. Mom hopped in the car, which was angle-parked in the High School parking lot, and tried to get the car into first gear … she ended up driving the 4 blocks to the hospital across a major traffic artery (an oxymoron in a town of 7,000 people) in reverse gear.

I guess she must have thrown a big fit while I was under anesthesia, because shortly after this incident, my brother decided to pull the transmission, again.

Anyway, Brother said he needed a hand (an analogy for a person to do the labor) to help him with the transmission. I was sufficiently recovered from my emergency surgery to help him with this task. He probably chose me over our sister because I was a little stronger. I told him I would need to put a shower cap on my head to make sure the oil didn't mat my very long hair. I mean after all, the phone MIGHT ring and I might actually get a date for Saturday night.

So, we went out to the driveway and I crawled under the car alongside of brother. He loosened the bolts that held up the transmission. He said, "You'll need to hold this up while I work."

If you have never held up a transmission under a 56 Ford, well, all I can say is your life is not quite as entertaining as mine has been.

Sure enough oil poured all over my face, ears, neck and back as the transmission left its place in the car. Wow, I had no idea that 5 quarts of oil was that much until I was bathed in it.

Brother needed, of course, to go get a different sized wrench, "Hold on, I'll be right back."

So, I held on. Actually I think I was pinned by the transmission and the concrete below me. I don't think I could have moved if I had wanted to.

Hilda Carpenter

It's important to note at this juncture that our father had instilled in us a tremendous work ethic of being a "good hand." I was bent and determined to make my family proud by holding an old transmission and trying not to drink 10/40W oil.

The popular boys (who were of course jocks) in my High School all had really cool cars. There was this one boy, Gene, who had a really cool fastback mustang. Another boy, Ed, had a really cool regular mustang, and then there was Steve, who had a classic, 1957 Chevy. I have no idea if my brother had called all these boys (who were in my class, one year below him) to tell them to come see his idiot sister, but one by one they all drove by our house. Each one stopping to ask brother what he was doing, and to ask him if he needed any help. About that time, they would look under the car and see me. It was humiliating but what was I supposed to do? I had a damned transmission on my chest and was covered in oil with a shower cap that had little flower appliqués all over it.

That was the last time I worked on Brother's car with him. None of the cool boys ever asked me out, hell they didn't even invite me over to their house to work on their cars.

Things happen for a reason, hubby loves that I understand mechanics, so I guess it all worked out in the end.

Rural Genius: Secrets to Long Term Marriages

Guys who are Girlfriends

When I first met hubby, I admit, I wasn't too sure about his sexuality. I mean his vibes were definitely "hetero" and his best friend was a flaming-gay guy. I really liked his best friend too. But then I've always liked gay guys. It wasn't until after I moved to California that my hairdresser accurately spotted me as a fag hag. There's just something wonderful about having a guy as a girlfriend. Or a girl as a guy friend.

I have since moved my horizons to realize that hetero guys can also be girlfriends. In fact, hubby is really my best boyfriend and girlfriend. I think that happens when someone is completely comfortable with his sexuality. Hubby is just as comfortable going to an art show as he is a football game, or a tool show.

In high school, I guess I had a lot of straight and gay guy friends that were better friends than any girlfriend that I'd ever known. For one thing, guy-girlfriends are honest, and they don't stab you in the back. Girl-girlfriends are vicious. Or at least that's how it was in the itty bitty town where I grew up. Plus, with the guy-girlfriends that weird sexual dynamic that pulls is absent. Without that sexual tension, there is just a lot of laughter and friendship.

Hubby and I had drinks in a San Francisco gay bar with his gay, best friend and 3 of his best friends. Turns out one of the best friends ended up being my hairdresser for 19 years—fantastic luck, right? Well, the waiter comes over to our table to ask for our drinks. I got to go first and I ordered a daiquiri, next his best gay friend ordered a Manhattan, the other two guys ordered Champagne cocktails. When the waiter got to hubby, hubby places his arm on an elbow in a John Wayne kind of movement and said, "Scotch, neat."

The other men and I started laughing as his best friend said,

Hilda Carpenter

"OOO so *butch!*"

After moving back to Texas with Hubby, most of my guy-girlfriends are still in California. So, now what I find is the guys who are 80+ years old are like guy-girlfriends, even if they aren't gay.

So, for all the poor teens and young adults trying to figure out relationships, my recommendation is get yourself some guy-girlfriends, or girl-guy friends, at least you know with them that there is hope for the human race.

Part 4 The 12 Secrets to Long-term Marriages and Relationships

Secrets of Long Term Marriages/Relationships

I have no idea if there are more or less than 12 secrets to a long term marriage, but there sure is a lot of research on it. Amazon publishes thousands of books that cover the gambit of:

Selecting the right mate

Getting along with the right mate

Divorcing the mate — and even

Survival after burying the mate.

In my extensive, personal (sic) research of going through three marriages, seeing many marriages fail, and succeed over 44 years, I've come up with what I think are 12 most-important secrets to having a long-term marriage. I present these to you based on absolutely no definitive research, other than my own life stories and stories of my family with successful marriages (meaning no divorce and they didn't kill each other), and unsuccessful marriages (meaning they did divorce & they didn't kill each other). So this last chapter is devoted to you who only read the last chapter of a book

Remember to read this with tongue in cheek — because this is how I am sending these words out in the Universe! The truth is, no one really knows all the secrets, the fun is finding your own secrets.

Rural Genius: Secrets to Long Term Marriages

Secret #1 Know Thyself

Determine if you came from a screwed-up family. If you aren't sure whether you came from a screwed up family, then count on it that you did. Most healthy families know how good they have it. In the book "The Science of Happily Ever After" by psychologist, Ty Tashiro, PhD, his research says people who were secure in their childhood will most likely join with someone who also had a secure childhood. Similarly, someone who was an avoidant child (think of these kids as the adult children of alcoholics)—meaning they simply resolve not to care too much. My dad would have phrased this as, "I'd rather be a disappointed pessimist than a disappointed optimist." Lastly, someone who was an anxious child, meaning they were overly clingy to mother, continued to be distressed even after they were comforted. These folks will most likely opt to marry another anxious child.

The question then becomes how do I recognize the secure vs. Avoidant vs. Anxious adult? Ok, this is easy: look at your mate's parents and how they interact with your mate. If they are comfortable and easy with joking, teasing, laughing and no one gets their feelings hurt (or if they do they can call "foul"), then most likely they are secure. If they are avoidant—they haven't talked to their parents in years, and the very idea of going to visit them to introduce them to their prospective mate, fills them with terror. For the anxious child, they'll blab on and on about how rough their childhood was. They'll say things like, "Mother always ignored me, but then she was a bitch."

Got it?

For those who are unfortunate enough to pick a partner whose parents are deceased, or unknown, then look at how that partner is with friends. This is a great indicator of his/her socialization skills.

Most people don't know that a healthy personality really doesn't stop forming until 25 years of age. My recommendation is for no one to marry before 25, you're still an adolescent and won't really know your own mind and preferences until at least that age.

In the long run, the secret could be centered in the statement, "Know thyself." Take your time in choosing a mate. I'm not talking about sexual partners. I'm talking about someone with whom you want to have a relationship. Take a year to 3 years to know them and their families. The important interpersonal data is there, should you decide to look at it.

Secret #2 Human Development Progression Pyramid

Renowned psychologist, Abraham Maslow postulated a theory that said human needs and development is based on a hierarchy. He represented this hierarchy with a triangle. Within the triangle each stage of development or need is based on the the previous level of the triangle.

The bottom (floor one) of the triangle is where all a human's physiological needs reside. So consider someone who is hungry, they will need a sandwich long before they will need sex. After they are fed, then they look for shelter, NOW they're ready for sex. Oh, they probably found clothes to keep them from freezing, too.

Floor two (going up the triangle) deals with safety. So, now they're fed, clothed, and sexed ... might be a good idea to find out how to keep the sabertooth tigers away. Ok, we don't have to deal with sabertooth tigers anymore, true, but safety is also personal security, financial security, health, and safety from illness or accidents.

Floor three is where we finally get to relationships. This includes friendship, intimacy (remember intimacy is different than sex), and family. So, you're safe from the sabertooth tigers, you're fed, you've had sex, and now you have shelter ... NOW you can think about intimacy, friendship and all the wonderful things that come from being with other people.

Floor four is where you discover esteem. This includes self-esteem, in other words, you'll drop back down the pyramid if you have low self-esteem, and this low-self esteem will pretty much screw everything up. However, if you're careful to take care of the first 3 floors, most likely your self-esteem, and your partner's will be intact.

Floor five. This is the best part of human development progression—Maslow called it self-actualization. In my daughter's school, they talked a lot about how each person has a unique potential. Self-actualization includes spiritual awareness and striving to achieve your own unique potential. Ideally, you have a mate who supports you in that effort. If not, yep you guessed it, drop back down that old pyramid.

So, in summary, a secret to a successful marriage or long-term relationship is to travel up those floors of the pyramid together, and recognize when your partner may have slipped back a floor—help them move back up.

Secret #3 Fight Fairly

Now, we've taken care to know our partner's roots, we have a framework for recognizing what floor of actualization that our partner lives. Secret 3 is a tool.

The tool is learning how to fight fairly. Women, in general, suck at this. Mostly women will use their "wiles," or another way of putting it is emotional manipulation, to get their partner to do what they want them to do. I'm not saying that men don't do it, they do, in spades. However, women are groomed from a very early age (particularly avoidant childhood women) to manipulate really sneakily. Then as men develop, they learn it from us girls.

An example is best served: Woman gets her feelings hurt— but doesn't tell her partner what hurt her feelings. Hell, don't blame the woman, she may not even know WHAT hurt her feelings. She's just very aware of a feeling of sadness or anger. She wants her partner to "read her mind."

So, the partner to these women needs to learn how to draw out what is wrong. This sounds really easy, but it is incredibly hard to do. The dialogue may look something like this:

Male partner: "Honey are you upset?"
Female: "No"
Male partner: "OK, just checking."

He is in deep doo doo at this point. Not only did he give up too early, but he dismissed any tonality that went with the answer of

Hilda Carpenter

"No."

It's not his fault, most men have a hard time hearing women, unless they are screaming their or God's name in the throes of sex. Then, men can hear just fine.

How could he approach the conversation differently next time?

Male partner: "Honey, I sense you are upset. I'm concerned that your feelings may be hurt. Would you like to talk about it?"
Female: "No" or she may say something like "I'm not upset, you're the one who is upset."

This little trick of turning the table is exactly that—a trick. What she's actually doing is trying to get her partner to fight, a means of getting his attention. OK the relationship is pretty sick, but I have a feeling you may have witnessed this at some time, otherwise, why did you jump to the end of the book?

Now for the silver bullet:

Male partner: "I clearly have done something to upset you. I really want to know what it was so I won't do it again. Please talk with me, if not now, tell me when you will talk with me about it."

Female:

Well, there is no dialogue, because if this is the first time you've ever muttered these words, she's completely blown away and has no response … be patient and repeat as necessary.

Rural Genius: Secrets to Long Term Marriages

Now, men ... oh they can manipulate too, often in the same way a woman does. In a recent Huffington Post column, Gail Gross, PhD cited fourteen points to fighting fairly. She says there's an old saying: a woman marries a man thinking that she will change him -- and she doesn't; a man marries a woman thinking she'll never change -- and she does.

Dr. Gross gives 14 guidelines on how to fight fairly:

1. To fight as an adult, we recognize that no one is perfect.
2. Find a neutral spot [to fight].
3. Simply and genuinely listen. Be there.
4. Open your heart and be flexible.
5. Be honest. Don't perform for approval.
6. When fighting using the empathic process, it is important to fight fairly.
7. Never fight on an empty stomach, or when tired or distracted.
8. Never personally attack your mate.
9. Don't read your partner's mind.
10. Honor the process [of fighting].
11. Keep your dialogue balanced.
12. Stay open to your natural self.
13. Never save stamps in a relationship. [Don't keep score]
14. Finally, if the relationship is out-of-control, immediately seek professional counseling.

The people who are in the most secure, successful relationships will recognize when things are out of control. You can typically identify if your relationship is off-balance when one or the other person feels like they cannot be themselves. I completely concur with Dr. Gross' recommendation for seeking outside counseling to help get your relationship back on track, or to learn how to fight fairly. For Hubby and me, we both needed separate counseling in addition to our couple's counseling.

If the relationship is out of balance, then at least one person may need outside counseling. Sometimes this out-of-balance situation arises when your children are going through a difficult period of human development, like adolescence. Or if there is a severe illness of a family member. Seeking counseling is not weak, it is a strong affirmative move.

Secret #4 Humor

The fourth secret is simple, don't take yourself or your partner too seriously. It is extremely important to have a sense of humor. This can absolutely be the magic bullet at the height of conflicts.

A suggestion? When you are in the middle of a grande fight, take a time-out.

Go do something fun, set a date for continuing the conflict. In other words, don't deny that you have an issue or conflict, but don't try to solve it in one go-around. A good phrase is: "We're not going to solve this today."

Even the healthiest couples have major conflicts. Some couples are loud, others are quiet in their conflicts, but bank on it, those conflicts are going to exist.

Realizing that a good sense of humor is critical to long-term marriage or relationship is a secret that you will hear from any couple who has been successful in their relationship that lasts over 20 years.

Sometimes, keeping a good sense of humor means that you just have to admit you are wrong—even if you know you aren't—and that your partner is right—even though you know they aren't.

Other times, keeping a good sense of humor means just that, don't be insecure, learn to laugh at yourself. If your partner thinks you are taking something too seriously, you may just be and it is time to lighten up about yourself.

Secret #5 Grief

There will be times in any long-term relationship where grief pops up. Sometimes this may show up as depression, or a natural reaction to something that is really sad that happens to your partner. Losing a parent, even if your partner was not close to the parent, will always, always generate some level of grief.

The key to remember is you cannot take the grief (what ever the reason) away from your partner. Be sensitive to their needs of additional attention, or their needs for more privacy. The need for closeness or privacy will be different for every individual. And, indeed the need may differ from various incidents of grief. Keep asking what it is they need from you, because depression and grief have great hiding places.

Organizational consultant, William Bridges, wrote a book called "Transitions" after his wife passed away. He was devastated and felt hopeless and lost. Out of this grief he realized that grief is a process. Whether that grief is imposed by a death, or a change that we weren't expecting, like getting laid off from work.

Bridges talks about this transition process as ending/neutral zone or middle/and beginning. A person will stay in ending for as long as they need before they even contemplate moving into a new beginning. Indeed, a person may actually start something new, then fall back into the grief of ending, cycling like a helix within the ending, neutral zone, and new beginning.

It is extremely important to understand that grief is not an incident, it is a process. Support your partner in ways that they need in their cycles of endings, neutral zone and new beginnings. The new beginning always happens, it just may take longer for some forms of grief than others.

Rural Genius: Secrets to Long Term Marriages

One little secret is that anytime anything changes, even if it is a good change, there is a loss of the old. Let's say that you quit your old job for a better one with more money and less time invested. The grief for the old job will show up as continually comparing the new, better job to the old one. When a person looks back at the old they are in a grief process. It is good to "count your blessings," so to speak. However, be careful to ward off too much energy pointed back at the past. Every time you think about the old job, especially with spite, you are in a form of grieving. In other words, you are revisiting the end, rather than focusing on the new beginning.

People who marry after a divorce will always have some form of grief. Hubby and I try to work at not looking at the past, but accept it that the past formed who we are today. Be grateful for your past, because this gratitude is where you gain wisdom.

Secret #6 Liar

There are many academic studies that indicate a professional can tell if someone is lying to them. The Business Insider lists 12 "tells" whereas a non-professional might suspect their partner is lying.

1. Changing their head position quickly is another one.
2. Changes in breath,
3. Standing very still,
4. Repeating words or phrases
5. Provide too much information
6. Touch or cover their mouth
7. Instinctively cover vulnerable body parts
8. Shuffle their feet
9. It becomes difficult for them to speak
10. Stare without blinking
11. Tend to point a lot
12. Shifting eyes down and to the left

But what about the times that it is kinder to lie? I don't mean to lie in order to cover up indiscretions such as infidelity, or tax evasion, or whatever you see as the most heinous crimes.

I'm talking about the time that if you tell what you see as absolute truth, you might hurt the other person with no gain in the relationship.

The best, most cliched example is: "Do these pants make my butt look big?"

If a person does ask this question, then you have two choices: first, give your rendition of the truth (i.e. You may think the pants make their butt look fat—but before you answer ask yourself something like: am I a fashion expert?). The other choice

Rural Genius: Secrets to Long Term Marriages

is to say, "I love the way you look in those pants." Now, this might actually be an untruth. However, in Western society we are enormously preoccupied with the way we look.

There is a reason we are so preoccupied. Marketing bombards us on a massive scale to get us to question our looks, our body image, whether we are having sex enough—you get it. In other words, why does your partner care about the size of his/her butt? In the big scale of things it doesn't matter, right?

Or does it? Ty Tashiro, PhD warns us not to fall into the trap of falling for someone for their looks. This form of narcissism (the process of choosing the other person is related to how good you think you look with them) is most likely going to result in a superficial relationship that will not stand the test of time. In these instances, the relationship begins with a form of denial or lie. We see this a lot in western society when a very older, rich man chooses a "trophy wife." Then, the relationship fails because either he died, or either one became restless and gave up on their commitment.

So, on some occasions, you'll need to lie to be kind. If you feel you really need to give the hard truth, then at least make sure your truth is necessary, truthful, pertinent, and kind.

Detecting lies in your partner is incredibly important. Many people are "surprised" by the failure of a relationship. When the relationship fails, communication broke down, lies or feelings were veiled from the unsuspecting person. How do you detect when your partner is living a lie? One way is to search your gut, use the 12 indicators as a guide, and most importantly, check in with each other. Retest your value systems to ensure they are still aligned.

Finally, if you are in a relationship where lies are commonplace, escape that relationship as quickly as possible (assuming even after checking in with each others' values the partner continues to lie). There is a pathology where a person simply is incapable of telling the truth. This person needs professional help, or you may need help to understand that pathology.

Secret #7 Substance Abuse

Substance abuse is a huge relationship-killer, unless the couple deals with it in a healthy way. This is where professional counseling, twelve-step programs, safe houses or even hospital intervention is key. If you are certain that someone in your family (spouse, child, friend) is in trouble, then a combination of Alanon and 12 steps, or counseling will help you navigate this treacherous road.

If your partner is abusing drugs or alcohol … you need help as much as your partner. Never think that it is only one person's problem. If you drink or use drugs daily and you find you are fighting more with your partner, most likely removing alcohol or drugs will help you get the relationship back on track. Take a vacation from alcohol and drugs for a month. Doing this will help in two ways. First, it will help you determine if you have a problem, because you will think more clearly. Second, if you find you get along better without the numbing effects of the substances, then it may be easier to give up the substances entirely.

So, the secret #7 is simple, keep drugs and alcohol, gambling, sexual exploits, and overeating out of your relationship. You may have made the most perfect mate selection in the world; however, these addictions can happen anywhere, seemingly at random to good people.

If addiction creeps into your relationship, then recognize if you are enabling your partner's affliction. If your partner says you have a problem, you do. Get help.

Secret #8 Sex

There are couples who abstain from adding sexual activity to their relationship until they have entered a contract, such as marriage, or co-habitation. I think it's a great idea, although I never did it that way.

What I found is that I learned a lot about the other person in the way they had sex with me. Were they kind, attentive, or selfish and disrespectful? How did they handle the relationship AFTER sex was done?

Your sexual decisions with your partner should be completely private. However, know that one of the secrets for a long-term relationship is to be able to freely discuss your sexual life with your partner. If you have a close friend who will listen, then talk with them about your sex life (assuming that friend is not the other sex and is heterosexual).

Friends can help educate you about what is "normal." Books are also a good resource for discovering your sexual preferences. I grew up not having anyone I trusted to talk about my sexual life. The one time I reached out to a friend, I ended up losing my marriage and running away with him. Hence, if your friend is heterosexual and is the opposite sex, this will lessen the intimacy in your private relationship. Find someone else to share your stories about your sexual life.

Sex will change as you age. This isn't bad, it doesn't mean that one of you have gotten fat and ugly. It simply means that part of your relationship has taken on a different tact. It may conversely mean that your sexual relationship is healthier as you age. Again, it is all very personal and private.

The secret is to always, always talk about your experiences with

Rural Genius: Secrets to Long Term Marriages

your partner. What did you like, what would you want more, or less? Communication with your partner in this very special area is critical. Don't let it take a backseat. If you are unsure about how to have these conversations, engage a professional therapist to determine your norm. If you don't like what you hear from the professional, hire a different one. If that one gives you the same feedback, then most likely you needed to listen to the first therapist.

Regardless of your sexual choices, sex should be fun. It's a normal, human function that should never be shrouded in shame.

All of this is true, unless the sexual dynamic is abusive. By abusive I mean that one person uses power to place the other person in a fearful, or shameful state. If there is abuse in the relationship, get out. Remember Paul Simon's Fifty Ways to Leave your Lover!

Secret #9 Ruts or Horizons?

"The horizon may actually be the top of the rut." I don't know where I first heard this, but I remember at the time I worked for Apple Computer. The significance of this in the business environment was to always challenge the status quo. Always check to make sure that if you have hit the status quo, then is it still appropriate? Business always needs to change to some degree to remain competitive.

In relationships, getting into a rut is really easy to do. Especially after kids come along, or a family member moves in due to financial or personal crises.

The hard part is breaking the rut without it feeling like the change to the rut is "staged."

Classic example: "To keep us from going into a rut, I think we should have a date night every week. Let's say on Wednesday."

The good partner readily agrees to this great idea. Then, Wednesday rolls around and they end up going to the same restaurant, or the same movie theatre. One or both of the partners is going to feel that the date night is really silly, or stifled or staged.

How do you make the Wednesday date night fresh each week? The answer is never do the same thing twice within settings. A date night can be a walk around the block, a canoe ride on the river, fancy dinner, movie that includes time for you both to talk about what you liked or didn't like the movie. Many couples will want to just get away from the kids and job, so a movie is the simple, quick fix. However, unless you engage with each other about "what" the movie meant to you, then you've wasted a lot of money on popcorn and hot dogs. These discussions help you

Rural Genius: Secrets to Long Term Marriages

discover more about your partner's value system.

Hubby and I decided that every other week we would get in the car for an "adventure." We took turns in setting up the adventure. Whoever set up the adventure hid the destination until we were in the car. After the car started, we told the other what we had planned for the hour, afternoon or day.

We did this even when the kids were at home. It was a treat for everyone and kept us fresh, adding new stories that we could share with our friends (who incidentally were very jealous).

So the secret is—keep the horizon the horizon, and not the top of the rut.

If you haven't done something different in more than a month—it's time for an adventure.

Secret #10 Spirituality

Secret #10 is pretty simple, really. Make sure you have a spiritual connection with your partner. Ok, not so simple indeed. If we reflect back to Maslow's hierarchy where self-actualization is the pinnacle, then spirituality (not necessarily religion) is at the heart of that actualization.

Keeping a spiritual respect for your partner is what I am talking about. Rejoice in their interests, celebrate their successes and even their failures. Why failures? Well, because that is where our character shines the most, where we bravely challenge ourselves to do something new. No matter what your partner's interest, hold it with a gentleness of spirit.

Our interests reflect our personalities, and hence, our relationships. Cherish each other's spirit. This one secret could take up a book in itself, I note it here as a reminder of how important our spiritual connection is to other people.

Some people marry their partner in their church, mosque or synagogue. Again, the spiritual value is what is important, not the religion. Marrying someone within your own faith certainly gives an indication of your partner's spiritual education. Then why do people who marry within their own faith divorce? The answer is about spirituality, the practice of those values in every day life, not a religious service.

Try to identify your partner's spiritual values, early and often. I say often because as you climb that Maslow triangle, your spirituality will naturally evolve.

Secret #11 Reflection

Practice reflection. This is very similar to the 10 previous secrets with a slight tweak. Set up time when you can give your partner feedback, or be a reflection as to how they are doing in your relationship, and not necessarily when you are in a fight.

Think of reflection time as an impersonal mirror. Your job will be to provide feedback on your partner's character. For example, "I was really proud of the way you handled —" or "Do you think you could have handled — differently? And if so, how?"

This is a simple exercise that promotes dialogue. Each partner must listen to their mirror reflection without defensiveness. The partner doing the reflecting must only give thoughts that are kind. If you are receiving the feedback, do not interrupt. A good practice is to write letters to each other. Partner A reads the letter to Partner B. Partner B's job is to listen, not interrupt, and after the letter reading is finished, do not argue about how Partner A's letter is wrong. The letter represents Partner A's perspective, or opinion, someone's opinion cannot be wrong.

The real secret to a long-term relationship is communication. Keep in contact with each other, so that each of you know what the other is thinking. Just like falling into a rut in actions, silence toward your partner (by this I mean that you have dropped the habit of letting the other person know what you think about their behavior) will result in a loss of intimacy that will permeate your entire world.

This is how people "grow apart" and are surprised to find themselves with a virtual stranger — they stopped reflecting with each other.

Einstein gives us the lesson, in his theory of relativity. Time can

Hilda Carpenter

be moved … distance can be overcome … and motion is simply a reaction based on an action.

What the heck did I mean by that?

If you reflect each others (action) you can create a reaction.

Following the secrets won't necessarily prevent heartbreak or infidelity or boredom or even bliss.

Take stock of where your relationship is, and always, always know that if you are in this relationship for the long run that what ever is going on in your relationship, good or bad, will pass.

Treasure each other and honor that time will move. If your partner reflected something that "hurt" your feelings, take stock, you just received a gift that will improve with time.

Secret #12 Affairs

The last secret is: If you are going to have an affair, particularly sexual affairs, then put a time limit on it.

I often see people choose to have an affair due to the intimacy that a working environment provides. Work, like the work of partnering in a marriage or long-term relationship contains very similar dynamics. For example, in a marriage you have similar goals. In a marriage you have to work side by side to raise kids, or advance your life's goals.

At work, these same requirements exist. Just because someone is married, it doesn't mean they are sexually dead to other people. Indeed, the intimacy of the workplace is ripe for the affair-dance. Most often the affair begins quite innocuously with little touches to the arm, back or other body part that is not explicitly sexual (bottoms, genital, or breasts). The affair-dance can begin with long-looks of understanding. Or, the affair-dance can begin with pheromones, those hormones we secrete when we are aroused.

If you find yourself in this situation, and a lot of my clients do, then the best thing you can do is to determine what you want out of the affair. For example, you may just want a good roll in the hay, release sexual tension from the tension of your job. Or, you may want to act out your fantasy with a co-worker.

I knew an executive who always conducted her affairs when she traveled to Europe. She had one-night-stands with other traveling executives, sometimes not even exchanging first names in the process. To her, this was simply part of business, a way to stay sharp. She never told her husband of her sexual escapades because they were simply meaningless to her. She felt no guilt and her actions did not negatively affect her marriage. Did her husband know? Well, I'm not going to tell you, but what I will tell you is there are two scenarios:

Scenario 1: She thinks she's getting away with it, but he knows. He decides to keep her secret (for what ever reason, e.g., keep the family together; she's nicer to him afterward, etc.). When this happens it is quite easy for the relationship to be on the brink. However, this practice also depends on the social norms of the society at play. In Europe the society is less parochial about sex. Thus, sex is typically seen as a physical not emotional act.

Scenario 2: She thinks she's getting away with it, and she's right. At this point, as long as she is evaluating the reason she chooses this behavior, e.g., examining her own self-awareness, she's probably ok. If she is in a society that shuns casual sex outside of the marriage, then there may be a deeper root than just a physical release. My suggestion if she were my client would be to suggest she look at the periodicity of her sexual experiences. Then, to look at any common factor among the men she chooses. This self-evaluation, when done with professional guidance, might uncover some personality flaws (see secret #1) that are hindering her own self-actualization, and are most likely damaging the intimacy with her partner.

I have only met a few people that can successfully have serial sexual exploits that do not damage the self-esteem of their partner, or themselves. In other words, from the perspective of a long-term relationship sexual affairs are most likely detrimental to the primary relationship.

When another one of my clients engaged in an extra-marital affair with his married subordinate, a dynamic of justification out of shame occurred. Let me explain. This executive's affair was completely out of character for him. Similarly, this married subordinate felt that the only "right" conclusion to the relationship was to end their primary relationships with their spouses. Then, they would be "free" to continue their own relationship with out guilt.

Conceptually, this is interesting, in actuality it was a disaster. The two affair-people might have a happy-ever-after ending; however, at least two other people are severely damaged by their actions. Even more people are damaged by their actions if they currently have children. Divorce is typically hurtful and messy. These two used their new relationship as a way to justify hurting other people. By the time they "justified" their love, they became blind to their and their partner's faults. From some level of shame, they were going to make it work. In the end, they were miserable.

The "justification" becomes a way that the affair-people can move quickly into another relationship without really examining if they even love each other. In the case of this executive, he only saw affair-partner in the best light, at work, or in a hotel. Clandestine liaisons are incredibly alluring and sexy. Getting up each day with bad breath and no break from each other is an entirely different can of fish.

Can a marriage survive after one person betrays the other? The answer is yes. However, my answer is a guarded yes. I say guarded yes because the implication of surviving a breach of confidence, break of a promise, is that there is a lot of work to be done by both parties to figure out what went wrong. It also implies a lot of forgiveness and a long time to rebuild the trust the couple once enjoyed.

Finally, the last scenario I would share is two separately married people who hooked up with their spouses' best friends, secretly. The result was a process of "justification", bliss, then after a year they couldn't really stand each other. They pointed out how the new partner was just like their old partner. In other words, they self-selected a mate exactly like they did the last mate.

The risk that the affair person takes is rolling the dice and coming up in the hole, so to speak.

So, the secret #12: If you are going to engage in an affair, decide:
1. Be mindful of why are you willing to do it? E.g., did you cover the previous 11 secrets thoroughly?
2. Did you have any qualms about having an affair before this one?
3. If your spouse or children find out about it, are they going to be hurt by your actions?
4. How long are you willing to risk your long-term relationship for this affair (by the way if the answer is more than a day, then you need to work on getting out of, or fixing your relationship with your long-term spouse BEFORE you have an affair).
5. Why are you attracted to this person: Intellect? Pheromones? Lust? Curiosity?
6. Then ask yourself what you think the affair-partner's answers would be to those same five questions. If the two of you are not in synch with your answers, then talk before you hop into bed.
7. Finally, try to talk to your partner about the fact that you are thinking of betrayal. This sounds a little weird, but oftentimes your partner may be more than willing to help change the dynamic so that you are no longer interested in having a relationship outside of your marriage.

Conclusion

Using the 12 secrets as a way to open up your relationship and discover each other more intimately is the gift this book gives you. The preceding life-stories are presented as a way to understand how the 12 secrets formed from my own experiences and observations.

My central theme in maintaining a long-term relationship deals with your own self-knowledge and your communication skills. My hope for you is that you continue to evolve your own self-actualization and that your partner will travel that path along with you.

Good luck and let me know how it goes.

—Hilda V. Carpenter, PhD

Made in the USA
Charleston, SC
17 June 2015